Pissing in the Snow
and Other Ozark Folktales

Pissing in the Snow
AND OTHER
Ozark Folktales

Vance Randolph

Introduction by RAYNA GREEN

Annotations by FRANK A. HOFFMANN

UNIVERSITY OF ILLINOIS PRESS

Urbana Chicago London

© 1976 by the Board of Trustees of the University of Illinois
Manufactured in the United States of America

LIBRARY OF CONGRESS CATALOGING IN PUBLICATION DATA

Main entry under title:

Pissing in the snow and other Ozark folktales.

Bibliography: p.
1. Tales, American—Ozark Mountains. 2. Erotic
stories, American—Ozark Mountains. I. Randolph, Vance,
1892–
GR110.M77P57   398.2'097'1   76-18181
ISBN 0-252-00618-6

To Gershon Legman

Contents

Introduction

As a graduate student interested in American regional materials, I studied Vance Randolph's Ozark collections along
with those of the other great regional collectors.* In 1971 I
took a job teaching folklore at the University of Arkansas,
knowing that one of the benefits of living in Fayetteville
would be the opportunity to meet and talk with Randolph. I
rightly assumed that I had much to learn from him, and I
quickly sought out Vance and Mary Celestia Parler, my colleague in folklore at the university, a notable collector in her
own right, and Vance's wife. We spent some happy evenings
that year talking about folklore, for Vance can compete with
the best of his informants as a storyteller. The tale of his years
of work in the Ozarks gave me a lively history of the discipline from a great collector's perspective. One of the most
fascinating parts of that tale pertained to the collection and
nonpublication of the so-called bawdy lore. I had not been
especially interested in such materials before—even though I
had heard of the "unprintable" collections from my professors at Indiana—but Vance's "history" so intrigued and an-
gered me that I determined to pursue publication for these
volumes. I could not believe that a major work by a dis-

---

* A shorter version of this introduction was published in *Mid-South Folklore*, vol. 3, no. 3 (Winter, 1975), in a special issue for Vance Randolph. Copy-
right 1975 by Rayna Green.

tinguished collector could go unpublished, and so I began my own commitment to this extraordinary collection.

Vance, having fought the battle for print through the years, felt unable to sustain the effort necessary to see the project through to completion. But, finally persuaded that a respectable publisher could be found, he agreed to allow me to act as his agent and editor. After arranging for deposit of Vance's papers at the Archive of Folksong in the Library of Congress, I took the manuscript with me to my new job in Massachusetts and began to seek a publisher for *Pissing in the Snow*. In truth, it was less difficult than the manuscript's earlier rejections by publishers might have indicated, though indeed, several editors still expressed doubts about the manuscript's content. Many distinguished folklorists—Richard Dorson, Roger Abrahams, Dell Hymes, Kenneth Goldstein, Francis Lee Utley, Herbert Halpert, and Barre Toelken—offered letters of support and suggestions for the publication of the volume. Frank Hoffmann, the acknowledged authority in Anglo-American traditional erotica, agreed to complete the notes which Vance had begun. And the editors and staff of the University of Illinois Press, noted in recent years for their fine publications in folklore, came forward with skilled and sensitive ideas for the presentation of the work.

Ideally, of course, the tales in this volume should have been included in Randolph's earlier books. They were collected at the same time and in the same way as the tales in the five volumes published by Columbia University Press in the 1950's, in fieldwork spanning almost four decades.[1] The

1 *The Devil's Pretty Daughter*, with notes by Herbert Halpert (New York: Columbia University Press, 1955); *Sticks in the Knapsack and Other Ozark Folktales*, with notes by Ernest W. Baughman (New York: Columbia University Press, 1958); *The Talking Turtle and Other Ozark Folktales*, with notes by Herbert Halpert (New York: Columbia University Press, 1957); *We Always Lie to Strangers: Tall Tales from the Ozarks* (New York: Columbia University Press, 1951); *Who Blowed Up the Church House?* with notes by Herbert Halpert (New York: Columbia University Press, 1951).

climate was not right at that time, however, for inclusion of bawdy material even in scholarly books, as Randolph discovered when he attempted to include bawdy songs in his major four-volume collection *Ozark Folksongs*.[2] His strong feelings about the inappropriateness of censorship and bowdlerization led Randolph to compile separate manuscripts of the folksong and folktale collections and of four other collections (about which more below). *Pissing in the Snow* was completed in 1954; after several attempts to find a publisher, it was deposited with the other collections in the Kinsey Insitute at Indiana University and in the Archive of Folksong at the Library of Congress. Several universities and individual scholars ordered microfilm copies for their own use, and so, even in the absence of publication, the work found a small scholarly audience. Ultimately, it achieved an "underground" reputation as the best and most comprehensive compilation of bawdy tales collected by an American folklorist. It entered the literature of folklore (always, incidentally, with the original and present title), yet its confinement to manuscript or microfilm deposit with restricted use in institutions or private libraries made it virtually impossible for all but a few to read the entire work.

As Randolph's correspondence indicates, many scholars knew of the collection in progress and contributed to a discussion of the material and the issues which its very collection posed to the scholarly and publishing world. Ernest W. Baughman and Herbert Halpert (who wrote the notes for several of Randolph's other books), Sidney Robertson Cowell, Josiah Combs, Alan Lomax, George Lyman Kittredge, Kenneth Goldstein, and others offered commentary on and references for the material, as well as advice on the publication of the material, should it ever be possible. Many sent variants of

2 Vance Randolph, *Ozark Folksongs* (Columbia: State Historical Society of Missouri and the University of Missouri Press, 1946–50).

songs and stories from their own collections, much smaller but just as unprintable as Vance's. The correspondence alone is a valuable document in the history of the discipline.[3] Of special interest is the correspondence between Randolph and Gershon Legman, the distinguished bibliographer and publisher of erotica who wrote to Randolph at an early stage seeking to publish some of Vance's bawdy lore in his series of traditional erotica. Eventually, through the manuscript/ microfilm center at the Library of Congress and the friendly offices of several folklorists here in America, Legman arranged to secure publication rights to all volumes but *Pissing in the Snow and Other Ozark Folktales*. Unfortunately, Legman has been able to publish little of the Randolph material; some appeared in his important psychoanalytical work, *The Rationale of the Dirty Joke*, and its sequel, the recently published *No Laughing Matter*.[4] But his willingness to see the material in print should, we hope, soon make publication of the other manuscripts possible.

The forthcoming appearance of *Pissing in the Snow and Other Ozark Folktales* marks a first for American folklore publishing in many ways. It is perhaps not surprising that, while some scholarship on traditional erotica exists, little field collected material has been published for use. As Frank Hoffmann notes in *Analytical Survey of Anglo-American Traditional Erotica*,[5] the scholar who wishes to study such materials may find little but frustration, since accessible printed works are often less reliable and authentic than field-collected lore, and since so much is available only in ephem-

---

[3] See Legman-Randolph-Goldstein correspondence on deposit with Randolph Papers, Archive of Folksong, Library of Congress.

[4] Gershon Legman, *The Rationale of the Dirty Joke* (New York: Grove Press, 1968), and *No Laughing Matter: Rationale of the Dirty Joke, Second Series* (Wharton, N.J.: Breaking Point, 1975).

[5] Frank Hoffmann, *An Analytical Survey of Traditional Anglo-American Erotica* (Bowling Green, Ohio: Bowling Green University Press, 1973).

eral printed and filmed form. But neither the ephemeral forms nor the other American field collections described in Hoffmann's survey are as comprehensive in scope, depth, and documentation as Randolph's manuscripts. In general, too, they are even less available for examination than Randolph's. Moreover, while two fine examples of "obscene" field collectanea have been published, one distinguished by its analytical perspective and attention to the social and cultural contexts of the lore, both represent lore taken from a smaller segment of a particular culture group than Randolph's. The publication of Roger Abraham's *Deep Down in the Jungle: Negro Narrative Folklore from the Streets of Philadelphia* [6] set the precedent for scholarly publishing that opened the door for such works as *Pissing in the Snow* and Bruce Jackson's recent collection of toasts from black informants, *Get Your Ass in the Water and Swim Like Me*.[7]

Until the publication of Abraham's book, even the *Journal of American Folklore* maintained the polite practice of substituting blanks for or Latinizing obscene words, even though several essays in the *Journal*'s 1962 symposium issue on "Obscenity in Folklore" spoke against censorship, Latinization, and bowdlerization.[8] Obscenity in folklore was, in fact, an issue that most early folklorists avoided. Many either refused to collect such materials (when informants offered them in the course of singing *all* the ballads in their repertoire) or refused to deal with them once they had been collected. Until Hoffmann began to repair the gaps in Thompson's *Motif-Index of Folk-Literature* [9] (where an asterisk—denoting "ob-

[6] Roger Abrahams, *Deep Down in the Jungle: Negro Narrative Folklore from the Streets of Philadelphia* (Hatboro, Pa.: Folklore Associates, 1964).

[7] Bruce Jackson, *Get Your Ass in the Water and Swim Like Me* (Cambridge: Harvard University Press, 1974).

[8] Symposium on Obscenity, *Journal of American Folklore*, LXXV, 297 (1962).

[9] Stith Thompson, *The Motif-Index of Folk Literature* (Helsinki: Suomailainen Tiedeakatemia, 1932–36).

scene"—substitutes for the written synopsis) in his *Analytical Survey*, folklorists' major tool for comparative work failed to be of use with bawdy lore. As we have previously noted, publishers declined to print such material when scholars collected it. Thus, little material has been available for study, and the small amount in print was censored to conform to polite tastes. For the study of Anglo-American folklore, the issuance of *Pissing in the Snow* marks a new scholarly beginning.

Vance took down all the lore Ozarkers gave him, from 1919 when he began collecting until the mid-1960's when illness forced him to stop fieldwork. The entire body of material, bawdy and non-bawdy, offers a picture of expressive behavior unparalleled by any other American region's or group's study. Though each specific item in the massive collection does not have the extensive contextual data that contemporary folklore scholarship demands, the whole of Vance's descriptive work in Ozark life and traditional expression places the bawdy lore in the largest context of life in the Arkansas-Missouri hills. Lest any readers think that the bawdy material solely represents the nature and character of expressive behavior in the Ozarks, let them consult Randolph's other printed works to place the bawdy in its rightful context. The dates of publication and collection indicate where and in what sequence it belongs in Randolph's other work. The six volumes, including *Pissing in the Snow and Other Ozark Folktales*, the two-volume " 'Unprintable' Songs from the Ozarks," "Vulgar Rhymes from the Ozarks," "Bawdy Elements in Ozark Speech," and the short collections making up one volume, " 'Unprintable' Ozark Folk Beliefs; Obscenity in Ozark Riddles; Latriana, or Folk Epigraphy from the Ozarks; Vulgar Lore from Ozark Children; and Ribaldry from Ozark Dances," should be intersticed with the whole multi-generic body of collectanea and analytical description which Randolph produced over the years.

The printing of bawdy lore separately from other Ozark traditions should not be viewed as any indication that the presence of the bawdy is more prominent than any other lore in Ozark life. Randolph says, in his introduction to the song manuscripts, "I do not believe that the bawdy ballads are more common in the Ozarks than elsewhere, or that the hillfolk as a class are especially fond of them" (i). Vance, reluctant to present an aberrant portrait of the people for whom he has so much respect and to whom the rest of us are much in debt, feared that readers would make that judgment if these materials were printed separately and not with other collectanea. Rather, the reader should realize that the other volumes, printed without these materials, offer the aberrant view of Ozark life. Again, Randolph says in his introduction to the folksong volumes, "obscene elements occupy a prominent place in American folklore, and should be accorded proportional representation in the literature. Everybody knows that bawdy songs persist in popular tradition. If a collection of folksongs contains no obscenity, it cannot fully reflect the taste and preference of the people" (i). Just as the work of Abrahams and those who printed obscene urban black lore helped to contradict the stereotypes inherent in the prevalent image of black people drawn from Br'er Rabbit stories, so this work will contradict some of the stereotypes drawn from Li'l Abner and hillbilly jokes. Too, the Ozark bawdy material should help to remedy the notion that only urban or imprisoned black males deal in obscene materials, a misconception easily derived from an examination of recent publications of bawdy lore.

Perhaps the unavailability heretofore of the harsher, more realistic, common, often obscene material accounts in part for one popular understanding of rural peoples as quaint, archaic, courtly rustics removed from the realities of life in a contemporary world. Certainly, bowdlerized children's tales and lore offer more of Disney than of Grimm when they omit that expression so common and dear to the hearts of children and adults. One has only to reflect on one's own childhood to recognize the limitations and false representativeness of most standard collections of children's lore.[10] The continued existence of bawdy folklore indicates that, regardless of attempts to censor what adults or children read and what publishers print, the material lives, circulates, and transforms itself in oral transmission. By keeping it out of print, we do not eliminate it. But by printing it, we do not give it a life it would otherwise not have; we only make available a fuller picture of expressive behavior to those who wish to have such a picture available. In a world deluged with X-rated films, bottomless bars, and leather shops, it seems rather quaint to defend a scholarly manuscript which contains stories some think naughty. Certainly, publication of Randolph's bawdy folktales will not be an attempt to capitalize on a ready market. It will be an attempt to offer scholars some "over-the-counter" data.

The material is representative of an important realm of life for most people, even if taboos which deny or operate against its relevance submerge it in waves of criticism. The lore collected by Randolph gives us clues to what people think about their own lives and language. Fieldwork tells social scientists that such lore is widespread among many people in America and the rest of the world. Its degree of visibility, its meaning in every society, and its contexts will have to be determined for every group and for individuals within groups, but its widespread presence and persistence can be verified by scholar and layman alike. Since the bawdy often finds expression in artistic forms—the same forms in which venerable ballads or religious tales are presented—folklorists find it of great interest. As folk art, it belongs to us as it does

10 Peter and Iona Opie, *The Lore and Language of Schoolchildren* (Oxford: Clarendon Press, 1959).

xvi

to those who produce it. As Horace Beck has said, "It is not in erotica, in folk art, in play party games that we are interested, but in folk culture. . . . Erotica is part of every society. Its form, its degree of prevalence set one group off from another." [11]

Many issues which arise out of an examination of the tales in Randolph's collection raise questions about bawdy materials as a separate type of folklore. For those interested in the style and structure of traditional genres, it will be tempting to explain the content of these tales in the light of their structure. For my part, in a comparison with various stylistic devices used in the tales and anecdotes Randolph had published elsewhere, I can find no appreciable differences. Since we are lacking the specific contextual data (when, where, by and to whom—ordinarily—what initiated and followed, and under what circumstances the tale was/would be told), we cannot really take note of the deepest sociocultural markings (tone of voice, type and response of audience, etc.) that would set these stories off from "clean" tales. But, as we have them, they appear to be indistinguishable in *stylistic device* from other funny stories told in the Ozarks and elsewhere. Overtly, bawdy *content* alone distinguishes them from tales with non-bawdy content. But the examination of structural components (the sequence of actions or descriptive segments, the kinds of actors and their actions), as well as a study of the stories as they are *told* rather than *printed*, may offer new insights into what tales mean in the cultures which produce them.

In terms of content, many motifs and themes common to the international body of folktales—obscene and otherwise—appear in these tales. The bawdy tales of the Ozark people show as substantive a connection with the international body

[11] Horace Beck, "Say Something Dirty," *Journal of American Folklore,* LXXV, 297 (1962), 195–199.

of Indo-European folklore as do the other tales Randolph has published through the years. Some motifs, themes, and uses of language compare to those appearing in that abundance of eighteenth- and nineteenth-century subliterary forms (e.g., *Fanny Hill* or *The Pearl*) and in contemporary collections having similar content. But some appear to be quite different; moreover, they assert their importance, if only through numerical presence. Some will be of great interest because they contradict or confirm certain presuppositions about the Ozark people's ideas and practices of sex and sexuality—a topic on which Randolph has commented throughout his published work.[12] While I wish neither to discourse on Randolph's perceptions nor to offer my own based on my study of Ozark folklore, some specification of major themes and motifs might help the reader grasp the nature of Randolph's bawdy folktales.

A theme (or belief) quite commonly expressed in contemporary academic folklore is the widespread notion that women do not enjoy sex. Its bipolar opposite, drawn from theological arguments peculiar to many religions, is that women are sexually insatiable. Freud, Mohammed, and the Pauline preacher would not recognize *their* women in the Ozark tales. Neither nymphomaniacs nor "frigid" women— in the extreme clinical definitions so favored by both ninteenth-century pornographic literature and medical science— appear in these tales. Rather, women enjoy sex as much as men. There are a few prudish, non-participatory women, but very few in comparison to those who enjoy sex and will go to as much trouble to satisfy sexual desires as men. Some women have little sexual education, but once they attain it, they learn and like their lessons well. In fact, just as many men

12 See especially *The Ozarks: An American Survival of Primitive Society* (New York: Vanguard Press, 1931), and *Down in the Holler: A Gallery of Ozark Folk Speech,* with George P. Wilson (Norman: University of Oklahoma Press, 1953).

lack sexual knowledge in the stories, and nearly as many men as women decide that sex is not all that interesting or worthwhile. From an examination of the tales in which male and female *narrators* and/or *characters* express attitudes, they view sexual prudishness and non-participation or dislike of sex quite negatively.

The sexual athlete or the stud so common to the boasts in black toasts and white rugby songs does not appear in the Randolph material. Some boasts and brags occur, but these are clearly marked as tall tales by the narrative devices in the story. "They used to tell lots of stories like that. . . . probably it is just a pack of lies," says the male narrator in "The Old Hole." Only one boast of a large penis is verified in a contest, but the possessor of the enormous organ let it be known that he thinks such "contests" are vulgar. Several men trick women into believing they have big penises, and several men go from woman to woman, but the emphasis is always on "good fucking" rather than on numerically high or extraordinary sexual feats. More common, in fact, than the boasts, brags, and successes are male failures. One man was rumored to have fucked several women to death, but the final judgment of all is that they died trying to get some "good fucking" out of his tiny penis. Men often try to convince women of their sexual powers and fail, or women remain unconvinced, with reason, from the beginning. Impotence, caused largely by old age or drunkenness, and small penises cause trouble because women do like potent men and large penises. No one condemns them for their preference, but people direct little more than a good laugh (rather than scorn and pity) toward the unendowed. In most of the tales, narrators and story characters place value on "good fucking"; in most cases they get it, and its frequency is thought to be beneficial to all.

In the entire collection, little of what takes place or few

characters, for that matter, could be characterized (in the culture's terms) as "sick" or "aberrant." They may be unfortunate, or they may lack good manners, good timing, or good sense. They may need a doctor or a judge to get them out of an absurd physical or legal scrape, but few need a psychiatrist. In fact, some "half-wits" fare better than most who think they are smart. Most often, the stories indicate that people need better manners or better sense. A few instances of what might be termed peculiar behavior fool the reader; consider, for example, the story of the old beekeeper who forced his young wife to lick molasses off his pecker when he had seven hundred pounds of strained honey in the house. It is his stinginess that the girl resents, rather than his desire for oral gratification, and the joke comes from the reader's surprise at the reason for her anger. Strange or ridiculous sexual encounters appear in small number, but they almost always involve an ordinary heterosexual encounter with comic physical action. The "missionary position" of intercourse dominates the sexual encounters, and the few mentions (often just acknowledgments that people do these things, rather than actual acts) of anal intercourse and fellatio receive little special comment beyond being noted as *different* from the usual form of intercourse. No homosexual act appears, and sodomy receives mention only twice. Masturbation, usually by women, occurs several times. The theme of incest will attract attention, since it is so much a part of the mountain people's stereotype. The Ozarkers themselves deal with the theme in their narratives, and its use in the tales indicates that they regard it as funny if not unusual. In any case, narrators know that non-mountain people and mountain people alike will think it funny, though the characters in the tales treat it rather matter-of-factly. Internal evidence indicates some ironic distance from the practice, though one cannot really determine whether the practice has tabooed status. A good deal of pre-marital and extramarital sex takes place, but rarely does either activity draw final condemnation or punishment. Men may get the clap; women may have to stop "running around"; a young couple may have to get married; but that is the worst of it.

Like European tales, these stories include a good deal of sex through mistaken identity, fortuitous accident, or pretended error, but characters display tolerance when the error is discovered. Much of the incest and extramarital sex is explained in terms of circumstances peculiar and unavoidable in the mountains—for example, the isolation of families or the practice of putting strangers up in the only bed and room in the house. A substantial number of tales deal with trickery, either in obtaining sex or in concealing sexual relations from others, but the trickery usually results in either a philosophical or a delighted acceptance by those tricked. Again, the tales involving trickery closely resemble European merry jests and anecdotes. Finally, some tales treat the scatological and urological—the literal dirt which people find both humorous, mildly disgusting, and embarrassing. These, like the stories where the humor revolves around the use of taboo words and the taboo acts of "sacred" people like preachers, or disliked characters like "uppity" women or men, merely reveal the widespread tendency to include the "unincludable" in the humorous repertoire. Scholars have often noted that sadomasochism appears frequently in British bawdry and that the French seem inclined toward the scatological. While the themes in Randolph's folktales may reveal something about the Ozark sexual character—either in the number of mentions or in the manner of narration—few indicate what anyone would call a preoccupation or preference in specific terms.

Few tales could be classified as intellectual humor and a number could be described as "low, bathroom" humor, but very few deal with anything that could be called "perverse" behavior, as Randolph himself notes in his introduction to the material. Moreover, the tales, though often absurd, are remarkably realistic as a whole. Many, in fact, describe believable human acts and reactions, though some might term the descriptions graphic beyond necessity. Compared with black toasts, for example, or with Native American trickster tales (such as those in the Winnebijou cycle), the tales do not appear to be products of a need for extraordinary fantasy, nor, I expect, would any judge deem them inspirational of fantasy. Moreover, the tales are rarely anti-social or perverse. Though some behavior draws censure or, more likely, amusement, it rarely draws malice and hostility. Even the fool often gets a fair shake here. Male and female, old and young, preacher and no-good—all receive similar treatment. Neither men nor women are described in the terms so common to nineteenth-century pornographic literature or to folk genres like toasts, rugby songs, or the dozens, and scholars may, in general, be surprised at the non-pathological nature of it all.

Like any other group of people, Ozarkers place taboos on speech and behavior. But, like any group, they make room in their expressive behavior for much that would be considered taboo in ordinary speech. In the introduction to "Vulgar Rhymes from the Ozarks," Randolph recounts an incident which illustrates this point:

> It is surprising to hear Ozark women, who are absurdly prudish in some ways and who would be insulted if a strange man pronounced such a word as *bull* in their presence, use very broad expressions in connection with riddles. I know a schoolmarm who sat with a bunch of hillfolk near Ft. Smith, Arkansas in 1928. There were both men and women in the group, and they told a lot of very suggestive riddles.
> In leaving, the schoolmarm said she'd like to come up

later in the fall and gather some nuts on the place. The whole group looked embarrassed and some of the men walked away. "Riddles is riddles," an old woman explained later, "and you can say anything *then*. But when you're a-talking sense, you don't never say nasty words like *nuts* in a mixed crowd. Leastways *decent* people don't, 'specially women-folks." (ii)

Certainly, as I have noted and as Randolph has often pointed out, the mountain people do have boundaries in speech and behavior, and some tales in *Pissing in the Snow* include narrators' comments on those boundaries. Whether the narrators' censure or approval should be taken at face value or should as often be read as mock serious judgments, we can only guess from what we know about narrative style in the Ozarks. When the narrator comments, with respect to pre-marital sex and parental disapproval, "Things like that always blows over in time, if folks have got sense enough to keep their mouth shut about it," I tend to take his judgment at face value. Condemnation for the young couple is as inappropriate to him as a "loose mouth." But "The Romping Party" deals with female mutual masturbation and an act of heterosexual intercourse through trickery; the narrator ends the story with a moral judgment from the mother-in-law of the girl who gave up romping parties, and I read some irony into his comments. "Her mother-in-law," he tells us, "says such things are foolish, and maybe sinful besides." Often the characters in the tale define what constitutes bad behavior or speech, and the narrator neither contradicts nor supports them. In "That Boy Needs Pants," the father slaps his pant-less boy when he climbs up on the table and drags his "tally-whacker" through the butter. The guests are too polite to mention the breach, but, as the narrator says, "Everybody took notice they didn't eat no more butter." Usually the narrator merely reports what the people in the story thought;

often enough, the story's characters got a good laugh out of the absurd happenings in the tale. In "Something on a Stump," the country girl cannot accustom herself to the vulgar teasing in town. "There ain't no decent people in this town," she says, "and I am going back to Sowcoon Mountain." Her replacement in the boardinghouse where she worked is a Horse Creek girl, who, the narrator tells us, is "used to town folks' ways, and . . . ain't so easily insulted." Implicitly, he approves of the Horse Creek girl's latitude and disapproves of the Sowcoon Mountain girl's prudishness. Yet, as with most of the stories, the narrator seems to enjoy the presentation if not the substance of both women's perspectives. Most tales are told in a kind of neutral way, even when the characters in the tale are not neutral. Certainly what many people—Ozarkers and outsiders—would term obscene, dirty, scatological, pornographic, and bawdy is in these tales. Contemporary Ozarkers might find this material alien to them. Of course, much of it comes from people who lived a number of years ago; as the heavily rural content indicates, they may have lived quite differently from succeeding generations in the mountains. Like the Child ballad collections from Appalachia, these tales may be representative of expressive behavior common as late as the 1920's and 1930's, but now far removed from what people sing and say. Moreover, this lore, like all other folklore, comes from individuals, and much may represent an individual's repertoire and not that of the group. The person who tells bawdy tales may be a unique and idiosyncratic person, just as the fine singer or storyteller of "ordinary" songs and tales is a unique performer. "Many country people never even heard these songs," said Rufe Scott of Galena, Missouri, of the bawdy tunes he gave Randolph, "but there is at least one fellow in every neighborhood who knows a lot of them" (i). And Randolph comments, "Some backwoods singers specialize in vulgar ditties, just as others prefer to sing hymns" (i). Surely there would be those who knew more bawdy songs or tales than others, and there would be certain people before whom specific other people could not repeat what they knew. There would be certain times when this material would not be deemed appropriate for repetition. Women might only repeat bawdy lore in the women's closed circle, or to male family members only, or to close, trusted male friends. Some kinds of material might be restricted to male groups only and often to the repertoires of young males in male groups. Some material might only be repeated by specific kinds of people at specific times, but the others would "know" the material, recognize it, and keep it in their passive repertoires though they might never "perform" it themselves. As an examination of the Randolph collection tells us, however, this bawdy lore came from a large number of people, rural and urban, male and female, and little of the material came from such "star" performers. Most came from people who performed or knew bawdy lore along with a wide range of other material (all published in Randolph's books). It is obvious (from the tale collection and from the rest of the bawdy lore collected by Randolph) that the bawdy material circulated widely among the population; that many who eschewed its performance knew of it; and that many who tolerated or engaged in its performance represented a much wider segment of the population than has been represented in other collections.

Obviously, the reasons for the disparity between the themes and tones of the Ozark lore and other readily available bawdy lore lies mainly in the differences between the groups whose expressive forms have been collected. But other reasons, perhaps more interesting than those cultural differences, should be brought forward. The discussion above indicates some of these differences. First, other collections now in print (some, like the Victorian materials, in reprint) have been drawn from restricted segments of social groups so that no complete picture of any one group's expressive repertoire has ever been made available for analysis. Most bawdy lore collected in the United States, for example, comes from *male* informants representing selective experiential segments of the cultural groups to which they belong. Young urban black males, fraternity members, members of the armed services, lumber-jacks, and rugby players do not comprise a representative sampling of their own ethnic, social, economic, racial, regional, or religious groups. They may not even represent their own gender group in some cases. What remains clear, however, is that large segments of the population, notably women and children, rural people in general, and white lower-class people, have been left out of the collections of bawdy lore.

Randolph's collection remedies the imbalance. Taken as a whole, it includes a good deal of material from women and children, mostly lower-class people, and all Anglo-Americans. Women told Vance fourteen of the tales in his collection. Perhaps the publication of these and other materials from women in the other bawdy manuscripts will offer scholars a chance to examine materials that they have otherwise not collected or examined. In the Ozarks and elsewhere in America, Europe, Asia, and Africa, women play an important role in the transmission of erotic lore. Hoffmann says that "little of this kind of material has been collected from women, on the assumption that erotica is primarily male oriented and of comparatively little interest to women" (77–78). As he suggests, and as many fieldworkers know, women circulate, invent, and enjoy bawdy lore in many cultures of the world. I have heard, for instance, versions of seven of the folktales in Randolph's collection from female relatives and friends in Texas. Not only women's but also children's bawdy lore contributes in these collections to a fuller understanding of the role of the obscene in larger contexts and segments of life. Here, obvious omissions from standard collections are restored.

The omissions of certain segments of the population from standard collections have as much to do with the nature of the collectors as with the narrowness of the groups from which they collected. Just as contemporary psychiatric/therapeutic models have been drawn largely from the intellectual and emotional perspectives of highly educated upper-class male Europeans and Anglo-Americans, for example, so have most collections of bawdy lore been done by the same kinds of people. Their restrictions have limited the kinds of material they sought and were able to obtain. Though Randolph was neither ill educated nor lower class, and though he was an outsider, he became an Ozarker by choice and adoption. The mountain people came to know him as a friend and advocate. He was a journalist, not a professor. And though he was male, the women came to include him in their circles as a trusted friend. Women gave him not only the lore of the granny women so rarely collected by male fieldworkers, but also bawdy lore. He talked both to the rural mountain people and to those who had moved to the cities. The breadth of topics and genres he covered in those fifty years of collecting, as well as the various kinds of people he persuaded to talk with him, tells us something about the uniqueness of the collection. That breadth of informants and topics should clue us to the representativeness of this collection for the Ozarks and should determine why this bawdy collection is so unlike others.

The role and function of the obscene, bawdy, and lewd in daily life and conversation—rather than in strictly defined "performance" situations—has received little attention from analysts, except for Abrahams's studies of black male performance. Clearly, Randolph's daily involvement in the mountain people's culture and lives paid off in terms of the fullness of description and the breadth of data he took down. Though some of what he collected resulted from his requests for "stories"—typical performance genres—much also came in the normal course of conversation. The folktales with the companion works, "Bawdy Elements in Ozark Speech" and *Down in the Holler: A Gallery of Ozark Speech*, offer a full portrait of ordinary *and* artistic speech. Thus the bawdy conversation can be placed alongside the non-bawdy. Furthermore, because of the very nature of the tales—most of them not "folktales" in the classic European sense, but anecdotes and jokes—the tales suspend use of language peculiar to folktales and so different often from ordinary speech. The people in these tales are not the princesses, witches, princes, and heroes of the elegant European tale, but more the common people of the merry jest, the salesmen, farmers, farmer's daughters, dudes, country cousins, old men and women, widowers and widow women, and preachers, plus the customary complement of half-wits and smart alecks that make up the daily repertoire of stock characters. This is bawdy lore from daily life, rather than bawdy fantasy as projected by film producers, college professors, literary figures, or psychoanalysts. How much more useful for us to study the "rationale of the dirty joke" from the perspective of real dirty jokes and dirty joke tellers than from some perspective drawn from models derived by people who neither create nor perpetuate them. Taking the above into consideration, I then urge the reader to believe that this material was known and appreciated by a wide variety of mountain people and to think that it might point to certain constructs and ideas important to Ozark life. But again, the bawdy lore should be examined with the rest, and it should all be examined in context for any determination of what it *means* to Ozarkers and what it *does* for them.

I warn readers against the restrictive and exclusive interpretations of this lore from the perspective of any model (e.g., Freudian, Marxist, Jungian, structuralist, Malinowskian). Perhaps all approaches could be applied sequentially if the reader wishes to weigh different ways of "reading" such material. But academic models may be inappropriate for the analysis of folk materials from the folk's perspective (unless the "folk" in one instance happens to be an academic group). We should search for the "ethnomodel" and attempt to read the material from the perspective of the people who produce, perpetuate, and use the folklore.

I have pointed out some aspects of the material that have to do with the people who told Randolph the stories and with the various themes and content of some of the tales. I have suggested areas where certain frameworks, customarily used to analyze such materials, fail to comprehend the substance here. I have also suggested certain kinds of questions which arise from this material and which ought to be put to the entire body of material; these apply to other kinds of folklore analysis as well. What I can never regret is that trip to Fayetteville, and it is a real pleasure to introduce this book to an audience ready to appreciate another of Vance Randolph's remarkable works.

February, 1976   —RAYNA GREEN

Annotator's Preface

In annotating this collection, I make no pretense of having been definitive. I have felt it more important to indicate how widespread many of these tales are than to enumerate how many times nearly identical versions have appeared in published and manuscript collections. I think the fact that a story, in parallel and variant forms, has appeared in a dozen published joke books and humor magazines (which are notorious for cribbing from one another) is far less significant than the fact that the story is also known in France and in Russia, and may even have a lineage going back centuries. As the annotations show, a surprisingly large number of these tales are known in other parts of the world, and many of them were recorded as early as the fifteenth or sixteenth century.

Furthermore, the nature of the stories is in itself an obstacle to massive annotation. Although earthy jests, anecdotes, and legends may have a long history of publication and may be represented in folklore archives all over the world, relatively few of them have been classified in the standard indices of folk narrative. Stith Thompson recognized the existence of an entire literature of sexual humor, but he considered it beyond the scope of his work. He simply left a gap of fifty numbers in Chapter X (Humor) of his motif-index for the future classification of such motifs.[1]

---

[1] Stith Thompson, *Motif-Index of Folk Literature* (Copenhagen and Bloomington, Ind., 1957), 514n.

The indices of erotic folklore which we have at the present time are incomplete and (for other reasons as well) less than satisfactory to work with. As part of my own study of erotic folklore, I compiled pilot type and motif indices of erotic folk narrative.[2] Their limitation is that they are just that—pilot indices. The types and motifs were drawn from approximately half of the *Kryptadia* collections, the five Randolph manuscript collections, and a handful of miscellaneous works. It was not my purpose to index the mass of material itself, but to develop a structure that could be integrated into the Thompson indices. I believe I was successful in accomplishing that, although as I use the indices, I find that I would make some changes if I were to do them over again. However, since there now exists an international committee concerned with revision of the motif-index (and possibly the type index as well), I think that all future decisions regarding the structure and content of both the original and any supplementary indices should remain in its hands.

Gershon Legman, in his two massive volumes, *Rationale of the Dirty Joke* and *No Laughing Matter: Rationale of the Dirty Joke: Second Series,* proposes and outlines a different kind of index of sexual humor—one based on broad theme rather than specific motif, and one that interprets and analyzes as well as classifies. Although I am not in complete agreement with his interpretations (basically psychoanalytical), I found his volumes invaluable references sources in that they include hundreds of illustrative examples from both printed and oral sources.

A few words about the notes themselves. The headnotes to the tales are entirely Vance Randolph's, both in content and wording. The annotations following the tales are primarily mine. In the original manuscript Randolph made oc-

2 Frank A. Hoffmann, *An Analytical Survey of Anglo-American Traditional Erotica* (Bowling Green, Ohio, 1973), pp. 160–288.

casional annotations; where these have been included, I have indicated that they are his. Ernest Baughman, of the University of New Mexico, read the manuscript when Randolph first put it together and noted parallel stories which he had heard either in Indiana or in New Mexico. These references, too, have been included in the annotations. At the beginning of each annotation I have given a motif number or numbers. Those placed within brackets are from my pilot motif-index; those without brackets are from Stith Thompson's motif-index. I had thought to include Legman's chapter, section, and subsection classification numbers as well. However, since he often makes reference to the same story in more than one chapter or section, I felt that such notation might prove more confusing than helpful, and that simple page reference in the text of the annotation would be best.

A special note of acknowledgment and thanks must go to both Ernest Baughman and Gershon Legman for their extensive contributions to the annotating of these tales.

December, 1975   —FRANK A. HOFFMANN

Pissing in the Snow
and Other Ozark Folktales

Preface

These stories were collected in the Ozark Mountains, where I have lived since 1920. I gathered hundreds of anecdotes, and published many of them in books and folklore journals.[1] The tales which follow were omitted from my earlier publications, because the editors objected to certain inelegant expressions.

There are, in modern American English, some twenty-five words which refer to the excretory and sexual functions. Tolerated in common speech, these terms are considered offensive in print. About twenty of them are taboo to the extent that they do not appear in ordinary dictionaries.[2] Some of these words are seen in popular novels nowadays, but seldom in serious publications. An anthropologist is free to publish a detailed description of any indecent situation, by using Latin derivatives instead of the vulgar English equivalents. But many folktales can't be presented in this academic jargon, because they depend upon linguistic as well as situational elements for effect. Translate a vernacular legend into the language of the schools, and it is no longer a folktale. An honest folklorist cannot substitute *feces* for *shit,* or write *copulate* when his informant says *fuck, diddle, roger,* or *tread.*

1 *Hoosier Folklore,* IX (1950), 37–48; *Southern Folklore Quarterly,* XIV (1950), 79–86; XVI (1952), 165–176; *Western Folklore,* X (1951), 1–10; *Journal of American Folklore,* LXV (1952), 159–166; *Who Blowed Up the Church House, and Other Ozark Folktales* (New York, 1952), pp. 232; *Midwest Folklore,* II (1952), 77–90.

2 Richard A. Waterman, "The Role of Obscenity in the Folk Tales of the Intellectual Stratum of Our Society," *Journal of American Folklore,* LXII (1949), 163.

3

Why should one employ such a noun as *penis*, if the narrator prefers *pecker, horn, jemson* or *tallywhacker?* Many of these stories are innocent, even childish, but they do contain vulgar terms like *cunt* and *twitchet*, therefore the gentlemen who edit the scholarly journals will not print them. Such tales are, however, an important part of our oral tradition. It is impossible to present a well-rounded picture of Ozark folklore without some obscene items.

The Ozark hillfolk seldom tell ribald stories in mixed company, as many city people do. They have their own ideas of propriety,[3] and are often shocked by innocuous urban conversation. The old-timers feel that sexual and scatalogical topics have no place in casual talk between men and women, unless the parties concerned are very intimately acquainted. Most of the bawdy tales which I have collected were told by adult males when no womenfolk were about, or by women who had mingled with outsiders. Such stories are not aphrodisiac, or intended to incite antisocial sex activity. They merely evoke laughter.

A few of the items in this book were recorded phonographically and transcribed from the playback. But in most cases I made notes in pencil as the narrator spoke and then typed the story a few hours later. Not one of the tales is a verbatim transcript, but they are all pretty close to the mark. They are not literary adaptations or reworkings. I have not combined different versions or used material from more than one informant in the same text. I just set down each story as accurately as possible, and let it go at that.

—V.R.

Eureka Springs, Ark.
September 20, 1954

[3] See my "Verbal Modesty in the Ozarks," *Dialect Notes*, VI (1928), 57–65. Also Randolph and Wilson, *Down in the Holler* (Norman, Okla., 1953), pp. 95–121.

4

1. Pissing in the Snow

Told by Frank Hembree, Galena, Mo., April, 1945. He heard it in the late 1890's. J. L. Russell, Harrison, Ark., spun me the same yarn in 1950; he says it was told near Green Forest, Ark., about 1885.

One time there was two farmers that lived out on the road to Carico. They was always good friends, and Bill's oldest boy had been a-sparking one of Sam's daughters. Everything was going fine till the morning they met down by the creek, and Sam was pretty goddam mad. "Bill," says he, "from now on I don't want that boy of yours to set foot on my place."

"Why, what's he done?" asked the boy's daddy.

"He pissed in the snow, that's what he done, right in front of my house!"

"But surely, there ain't no great harm in that," Bill says.

"No harm!" hollered Sam. "Hell's fire, he pissed so it spelled Lucy's name, right there in the snow!"

"The boy shouldn't have done that," says Bill. "But I don't see nothing so terrible bad about it."

"Well, by God, I do!" yelled Sam. "There was two sets of tracks! And besides, don't you think I know my own daughter's handwriting?"

[X717.3.1]
   Ernest Baughman notes that he heard the tale in Albuquerque in 1952. A similar tale may be found in Lockridge, *Waggish Tales*, pp. 85–91. Legman, *Rationale*, II, 851, gives a version

heard in the United States in the 1930's and in London in 1953, in which the mother recognizes the daughter's handwriting. He also notes a variant form, heard in New York in 1940 and again in 1942, with homosexual implications, in which one man asks another to hold and direct his penis because he can't spell.

The story, as given here, has two essential elements: the fact that the boy's pissing in the snow spells out a name, and the father's recognition of his daughter's handwriting. The tale is usually structured as a joke, with the revelation of the girl's handwriting as the punch line. This structure is weakened in the Lockridge version, in that the irate father insists that the handwriting is that of his daughter's lover rather than that of the girl.

In recent years, the story has had renewed currency, adapted to the structure of the "there's some good news, and there's some bad news" joke. In this form it is used as a put-down on a well-known political figure who is informed of the act as a means of getting rid of an unwanted colleague (the good news), and then of the fact that the handwriting is his wife's (the bad news). See *Western Folklore,* **XXXIV,** 3 (July, 1975), 240–241.

2. The Pride of Durgonville

Told by Ernest Long, Joplin, Mo., August, 1930. He said it was a true story, related by a salesman from Anderson, Mo., in 1929.

One time there was a business man that got the agency to sell automobiles, and he was the biggest booster for miles around. He claims our town is the best place to live in the whole goddam state. If we all get behind the Commercial Club, he says, and put our shoulder to the wheel, we could sell more goods than Joplin and Springfield put together. But everybody has got to cut weeds, and clean up their yard, and paint their house, so the people can see how progressive we are.

That fellow sure did practice what he preaches, too. He had a fine brick building with big windows, and electric lights. There was a little office in front, where he could set behind his desk and see everything. He didn't have no common privy, neither, but a fine water-closet right inside the building. One day there was a salesman from Kansas City went back there to take a leak, and he begun to laugh. The business man wanted to know what is the joke, and the salesman says somebody has been a-writing on your wall.

"Yeah," says the business man, "It's hard to keep things clean in strawberry season. For about three weeks our little city is full of berry-pickers from up North, and they are a trashy lot." Him and the salesman went back to the restroom, and this is what some fellow had wrote:

> Some come here to sit and think,
> Others come to shit and stink,
> But I come here to pull my pud,
> Cause the cock in this town ain't no good.

The salesman just laughed, but the business man swelled up like a turkey gobbler. "It's a outrageous falsehood!" says he. "Why, we've got just as good fucking as you'll find anywhere on God's green earth! And when it comes to prices—"

The fellow from Kansas City just laughed louder than ever when he heard that. The darn fool was still a-giggling when he got in his car and drove off. But us home folks never could figure out what that salesman was laughing at. There wasn't nothing to it, only some lousy berry-picker coming into people's toilets, and writing dirty words on the wall. What's so goddam funny about that?

[X749.1.1]
Randolph gave this tale to George Milburn in 1933. Milburn intended to use it in a book (possibly a prose collection to complement *The Hobo's Hornbook,* 1930), but apparently it was never printed.

This obviously falls into the category of *blason populaire*, insults to a community or locality, an art perhaps more highly developed in the Old World than in the New. In the United States, such insults ordinarily focus on obvious characteristics like the community's weather, its restaurants, or its hotels. But certainly a community's girls are of primary concern to traveling salesmen or servicemen, who traditionally look for the amenities of female companionship. Only once, during a visit to a small southern town in the mid-1960's, do I recall a local business man vigorously extolling the fucking in the community.

3. Fireworks under the Bed

Told by Mrs. Marie Wilbur, Pineville, Mo., April, 1930. She had it from Mrs. Lucinda Mosier, also of Pineville, who heard the story about 1885.

One time there was a girl that was going to get married, and the man thought she was a pure virgin. But the truth is that she wasn't nothing of the kind. The girl got kind of worried about it, because maybe the fellow would raise hell when he found out. So she went to see a granny-woman, and give her two dollars. The old woman says, "Don't you worry your pretty head, because men are all fools, and everything will turn out fine."

The granny-woman give her a little tin snapper, so that when you push the top it will give a good loud click. "The first night you and him get in the bed," says the old woman, "just hold this thing in your right hand. Soon as he gets to going strong, just give a little yell and push the top. When he hears that click, he'll think it is your maidenhead a-popping." And so the girl says she will do it.

The contraption might have been all right, only there was another girl found out about the snapper, and she put one of these giant-powder caps inside of it, just to make trouble. When the fresh-married couple got in the bed, the bride give a yell just like the granny-woman told her. But when she pushed the top of the snapper it went off loud as a gun, and like to have blowed both of 'em clear out of the bed. The whole place was full of smoke, with everybody a-yelling at the top of their voice, and hell to pay generally.

When things finally quietened down, the folks figured that the neighbor boys must have set off some fireworks under the bed. People used to play jokes like that sometimes, when anybody got married, and they didn't mean no harm by it. The young fellow was so rattled he forgot all about maidenheads, so maybe everything turned out for the best. Him and her raised a fine big family, and you might say they lived happy ever after.

[X722.2.2]
This story is part of a substantial body of tales and jokes concerned with deception on the wedding night to cover up the loss of the girl's virginity. At the core of such stories is the semi-myth of the physical maidenhead, which has taken on undue importance as the indicator of a girl's virtue on many levels of our culture. There are still men who expect to encounter and break a physical obstacle ("pop the cherry") in intercourse with a virgin.

Number 78 in this collection, "First Time for Trudie," approaches the deception from another point of view, as does a story in Lockridge, *Waggish Tales*, pp. 176–180. It is also given in *Kryptadia*, VII, 4–5 (from Belgium). Legman, *Rationale*, II, 455–456, notes several other versions from the United States, and points out that the basic motif appears in Italian Renaissance stories as early as the sixteenth century.

4. She Didn't Like Molasses

Told by Mrs. Ethel Barnes, Hot Springs, Ark., April, 1938. It was a common story in Garland County, Ark., she says, about 1895.

One time there was an old bachelor that had a hundred hives of bees out back of his house. He never done no work at all, except put the honey in little buckets and sell it to the tourists. For a long time he lived by himself and done his own cooking. But finally a young peckerwood girl named Roxie come over to keep house for him. The old man was awful tight with his money, and Roxie was always a-hollering because he wouldn't buy her no good clothes.

Roxie come a-walking into town one day, and she says the old man ought to be arrested. "What's he done?" says the sheriff. "He ain't done nothing, that's the trouble," says Roxie. And then she begun to tell how the old man won't get her no perfume, or lipstick, or even face powder. He makes her scrub the floor with sand, to save soap. He won't buy her a washboard even, and the cookstove is broke, and so is the window glass with a dirty rag stuck in the hole. He won't buy no lace curtain, but all the neighbors have got fine curtains in their window. Also her best dress is wore out, and holes in the stockings, and only two pair of shoes, and something has got to be done about it.

"Well, I'll talk to the old man," says the sheriff. "But probably it won't do no good, because he's got the name of being pretty stingy."

"Stingy ain't the word for it," says Roxie. "Why, every night the old bastard puts molasses on his pecker, and makes me lick it off. Common old sour molasses. And he's got seven hundred pounds of strained honey, right there in the house!"

[X736.2.1.1]
The association of food and eroticism is a long-standing one. Literature often has made use of eating to create an erotic atmosphere, as in the famous eating sequence in Fielding's *Tom Jones*, or, more recently, in the turkey-gorging episode in Chester Himes's *Pinktoes*. Explicitly erotic literature, such as this, utilizes food more directly. Paralleling this story is one of Randolph's *"Unprintable" Songs from the Ozarks*, in which molasses or honey is used on the male organ to make a "yaller gal" lick or suck it. Commercial stag films often depict a person eating or licking cream cheese, whipped cream, or syrup from a partner's body (*e.g.*, "The Maid Is Made").

5. Why God Made Stickers

Told by Mrs. Ethel Barnes, Hot Springs, Ark., March, 1938. She had it from relatives who lived near Hot Springs in the early 1890's.

One time there was a drummer wanted some gravels for his goose, but he couldn't find nothing only a girl named Lizzie that worked in the tavern. The folks told him Lizzie wasn't much good, because she aint' got no spring in her tail, and nobody likes a woman that just lays there like a turd in a dead eddy. But poor nooky is better than none, and travelers has to make the best of it. Soon as the supper dishes was done, him and her walked out to the pasture back of the corncrib.

When they laid down on the ground Lizzie acted kind of sleepy, but soon as the drummer climbed aboard she just went plumb crazy. You never seen such wiggling and kicking and flouncing around in your life. She give several loud yells too, but the fellow stayed right in there till his gun went off, and then he let her up. "My God, Lizzie, you're wonderful!" says he. The girl didn't pay him no mind, but just stood there with both hands behind her. Come to find out, Lizzie had stuck her ass down in a bunch of cockleburs. That's what made her so brisk and lively.

Lizzie spent most of the night a-grumbling, and putting witch-hazel on her bottom. But the drummer was feeling fine, and he says, "I never could understand why God made weeds with stickers on 'em, but I see it now." There was a story went round how he always carried prickles in his buggy after that, and the folks claimed you could trail him clear across the country. Whenever they come to a town where the girls have all got scratches on their ass, the boys knowed that drummer has been there with his goddam cockleburs.

[X735.2.1]

Legman, *Rationale*, I, on several occasions makes reference to the sexual partner who is so passive during intercourse as to be indistinguishable from one dead. One logical line of development into joke form is that of unintentional necrophilia, in which a man is brought to court for screwing his wife, who had been dead for several hours. He pleads ignorance of her death, claiming that she'd reacted to his advances in the same manner for the past twelve years (Hall, *Anecdota*, I, No. 429).

However, jokes on necrophilia, intentional or inadvertent, are rather strong fare for many people, and the alternative line of joke development is that of the fortuitous accident which forces the girl out of her passivity, as in this tale. I recall reading a related story many years ago in a men's magazine (specific source unfortunately not recorded). A girl who has no interest in sex finally agrees when the man buys her a pair of shoes which she desires. She wears the shoes to bed, and the man receives an unexpectedly good screwing as she twists about to admire them.

6. Betsey and the Mole Skin

Told by Bob Wyrick, Eureka Springs, Ark., May, 1951. He heard it near Green Forest, Ark., about 1910.

One time there was a fellow going with a pretty schoolmarm named Betsey, and they was the lovingest couple you ever seen, only he done considerable grumbling. The trouble was that Betsey liked to play with his pecker, but she wouldn't let him get it in her very often. She says that diddling is sinful, and ain't much fun anyhow. "Listen, Betsey," says he, "a man's tool needs oil every so often, or else it will turn on him like a wild varmint." But the schoolmarm just laughed, and she says that's nothing but superstition, which all educated people have give it up long ago.

A girl like that will run a man crazy, so finally he went to see Gram French. The old woman told him what to do, so then they killed a mole and skinned it. The fellow put the mole skin on his pecker, and it fit like a glove, with the sharp teeth sticking out in front. That night him and the schoolmarm went a-walking, and soon as Betsey got her hand in his britches she begun to cry. The fellow just lit a match and showed her how it was, and he says "I am going to the doctor tomorrow and have a operation." The schoolmarm figured he was ruined forever, and she knowed it was all her fault.

So then the fellow went to town, and stayed two or three days. When he got back his family organ was good as new, because he had took the mole skin off. Betsey was mighty happy about him being cured, and she says we better not take no chances from now on, and I will do whatever you say. So the schoolmarm give him all he wanted after that, and they never had no more trouble.

[K1352.1]

Stith Thompson, in his *Motif-Index*, lists a variety of means by which a girl is wooed or won by a trick (K1350), to which category this tale belongs. Old Gram French, who suggests the trick, also belongs to a long line of grannies who traditionally advise and assist frustrated swains in gaining the objects of their desires. Often in such tales the girl mocks her would-be lover, but through a trick ultimately is made to submit to him (Afanasiev, *Stories,* pp. 156, 160, 164, 173).

The toothed mole skin suggests a reversal of the motif of the "vagina dentata" (Thompson, *Motif-Index,* K1222), in which the man is tricked into believing the girl's vagina is toothed.

7. He Done It with a Bucket

Told by Mrs. Bertha Combs, Kansas City, Mo., December, 1932. She had it from relatives near Rocky Comfort, Mo., in the early 1900's.

One time there was a boy got arrested for screwing a girl, and they claimed he done it standing up, behind the door at the schoolhouse. But the girl stood pretty near six foot tall, and the boy was a little bit of a runt. The Justice of the Peace says he don't see how the boy could reach high enough. The people said he done it with a milk bucket. The constable fetched the biggest bucket in town and made the boy stand on it, but he still lacked a foot. So the Justice of the Peace says the whole case looks fishy to him, and they turned the boy loose for lack of evidence.

After the whole thing blowed over, the girl told some of her friends what really happened. "We was both standing up," she says, "and it was the damndest fucking I ever had in my life!" The ladies all wanted to know how little Johnny could reach that high. The girl just laughed. "The little booger put the bucket on my head," she says, "and then he hung onto the handle like a woodpecker!"

[X735.3.1]

The ludicrous situation of a little man (sometimes a midget) violating a tall girl in a standing position occurs regularly in folklore. Generally it takes one of two forms. In one, the girl is made out to be complaisant, for when the judge questions her closely about how the attack could be effected, considering the disparity in heights, she admits that perhaps she did stoop a little (*Kryptadia*, IV, 342 [from Belgium]; *Kryptadia*, X, 118 [France]; Hall, *Anecdota*, I, No. 281). In the form given here, the man is made out to be more aggressive, in that he puts a bucket over the girl's head and hangs onto the handle. Legman also heard this version, in New York in 1942 (*Rationale*, I, 95–96).

8. Billy Fraser Got Stuck

Told by Wiley Burns, Joplin, Mo., May, 1931. "It was something that happened to my wife's nephew," said he, "in 1894 or 1895."

One time young Billy Fraser went to see Judge Patterson's daughter, and it just happened everybody had gone out somewhere, so him and the girl was a-laying on the sofa in the front room. All of a sudden the folks come back unexpected, and caught 'em in the act. There was the judge and his wife a-standing right in the doorway.

It was the girl that seen them first, and she tried to push Billy off, but it wasn't no use. She was scared pretty near to death, and her twitchet drawed up so tight he couldn't get his pecker out. There they was, stuck together like two dogs in the street. The Judge was going to kill 'em both, but the old woman grabbed the pistol out of his hand. She says this is the terriblest thing ever happened in the world, and the whole family is disgraced forever, but it won't do no good to shoot somebody. "We got to hush this up," she says, "to keep down scandal." So they locked the doors and shut the window blinds.

The old folks tried to prise them two apart, and they poured on cold water, but it didn't do no good. The Judge was all for cutting Billy's pecker off, but finally he went after Doc Holton. When Doc got there he give the girl some medicine with a syringe, and told her to lay still. In about four minutes she kind of loosened up, and out come Billy's pecker, slick as a whistle. So then the boy run down the street like he was going to a fire, without even stopping to button up his pants.

The old woman was still hollering how the disgrace will kill her, and the Judge begun a-threatening what would happen to Doc if he ever breathes a word of it. Doc just looked at them contemptuous. "If I'd been loose-mouthed twenty years ago, you two wouldn't be married now," says he. "Just think that over, before you raise hell with these young folks." So then Doc picked up his little satchel and walked out of the house.

The Judge and his wife just set there a-looking at each other, but they didn't have no more to say. They never did make Billy Fraser no trouble, neither. Things like that always blows over in time, if folks have got sense enough to keep their mouth shut about it.

[X712.1.1.1]

Randolph notes having heard this tale a dozen times, in Missouri, Arkansas, and Oklahoma, and that it was always related as the truth, usually a recent occurrence, with names and dates. He makes further reference to the concept of vaginal contraction in Gould and Pyle, *Anomalies and Curiosities of Medicine,* p. 512. Ernest Baughman reported to Randolph that he had heard the story in Indiana, from a Connecticut source.

Legman, *Neurotica,* IX (1952), 52–53, and in *Rationale,* I, 212, relates the idea of a man and a woman locked in coitus because of a vaginal spasm occasioned by fright to the theme of the "vagina dentata." He gives further references in *Rationale*, II, 427–428, including one supposed to have taken place at the University of Michigan in the winter of 1935–36.

Although attribution is made to a different physical cause, Number 79 of this collection, "Cora and the Bottle," would appear to be a related tale.

9. The Old Tanner

Told by William Hatton, Columbia, Mo., July, 1929. He heard the tale in Lawrence County, Mo., about 1905. In May, 1950, I collected a similar item at Eureka Springs, Ark., from a man who said it was a true story.

One time there was an old man come to this town, and he was part Cherokee. The folks let him batch in an old shanty down by the blacksmith shop, and he run a tannery. People used a lot of leather in them days, and that old man could make the prettiest buckskin you ever seen. He took the hair off with ash-hopper lye, and then soaked the hide in oak-bark and stuff like that.

Some of the town smart-alecks used to make fun of the old tanner, because they figured he didn't know much. A bunch of the boys was standing around the stove one day, and Tom Gilmore come a-walkin in. "Can you tan hide with the hair on it?" says he. The old man just nodded his head. "Well," says Tom, "I got a piece of skin at home, that ain't no bigger than your hand. I've been a-working on it for twenty years, and it still ain't what you could call leather."

The boys all grinned, but the old man just stared at Tom Gilmore. "You fetch that skin down here," says he, "and leave it all night. I'll tan it, easy enough. And I won't charge you a cent." Tom looked kind of set back when he heard that, but the old man never cracked a smile. Pretty soon Tom Gilmore walked out, and the boys all laughed like fools. It was kind of a joke around town for a long time, and everybody would laugh when they thought about what the old tanner said to Tom Gilmore.

[J1643]
Everyone harbors the wish that he can be ready with an appropriate rejoinder when someone attempts to pull his leg or make him the butt of a joke. The large subsection of "Clever Practical Retorts" in Thompson's *Motif-Index* (J1500–J1649) is an index to the quick-wittedness of the folk mind in turning the tables on the would-be perpetrator of an embarrassing, awkward, or foolish situation. In this instance, the clever response of the old tanner puts Tom Gilmore out of countenance by implying that the old man could achieve overnight what Tom has been unable to attain in twenty years: the sexual mastery of Tom's wife.

10. Jack and His Family

Told by J. H. McGee, Joplin, Mo., July, 1934. He heard it near Sparta, Mo., in the early 1900's. Mr. McGee changed his voice from bass to falsetto as the brother and sister spoke; he told the story deadpan and earnestly, without the least trace of merriment. In 1950 I collected similar items from Bob Myrick, Eureka Springs, Ark., and J. I. Russell, Harrison, Ark. In Mr. Russell's version the girl says, "Your prick is considerable bigger than Paw's," and the boy answers, "That's what Maw says."

One time the folks had went to town, and there was nobody home but Jack and his sister Jenny. Jack was fifteen years old, and Jenny must have been about seventeen. It was a terrible hot day, so the boy took off all his clothes and laid down on the floor. There was enough cracks to let a little air come through, so it was the coolest place in the house. Jenny didn't have but three things on, and two of them was hair-ribbons. Him and her got to talking about one thing and another, so pretty soon she pulled her dress off and laid down beside Jack.

They just kind of petted each other at first, but then Jenny got to playing with Jack's pecker. It swelled up surprising, and she says, "My goodness, I never seen anything so big only on a jackass, and maybe that's how they come to name you Jack!" The boy didn't return no answer, and pretty soon she says, "Do you reckon you could stick that big thing in me?" Jack says there is only one way to find out, but maybe you better put a little grease on it first. So that's what she done, and everything worked out wonderful.

"My God, Jenny," says Jack, "I never had it so good in my whole life! Why, you're lots better than Maw!" The girl just wiggled her ass, and started to tickle Jack's balls some more. "Yeah," she giggled, "that's what Paw always says."

[X739.4.1]
There are endless variations on this story, with the dialogue assigned to different combinations of family members. Ernest Baughman informed Randolph that he had heard it in Indiana about 1935. In March, 1963, it was collected by Robert Adams in Martinsville, Ind., in the course of his field research for a master's thesis on jokes based on rural characters and rural situations. Further versions may be found in Hall, *Anecdota*, I, No. 225, and II, No. 37. Legman, *Rationale*, I, 96, notes that the earliest known version is in a 1912 manuscript by W. L. McAtee, who claims to have heard it in Grant County, Indiana, in the 1890's. In *Rationale*, II, 318, Legman says he also heard it in London in 1954, and further points out that it is often related as the dirtiest story the teller knows.

Although Randolph's informant "told the story deadpan and

earnestly, without the least trace of merriment," we should not be thrown off, for the implied humor is almost too obvious. Apart from the southern mountaineer's well-known manner of telling jokes with a straight face (a style, of course, shared by many others), one cannot miss the implicit humor in the characters' names. "Jack" is explained in the text, when his sister observes that his pecker is as big as that of a jackass (also known simply as a jack). Unexplained, however, is the fact that the sister's name, Jenny, is the generic name for a female donkey.

11. The Rich Man's Daughter

Told by Lewis Kelley, Cyclone, Mo., August, 1931. He says the story was known near Pineville, Mo., in 1886.

One time there was a rich man had a pretty daughter, but she was terrible sassy. The old man says the first fellow that out-talked that girl could marry her, but it looked like the town boys didn't have no chance. Whenever a boy come a-sparking she would make him look foolish, and then laugh right in his face. Or else she would begin to tell dirty stories. Back in them days, young men wasn't used to hearing blackguard talk from nice girls, and they didn't know what to make of it. Most of 'em just turned red in the face, and then they would hurry off down the road.

Finally a big country boy come along, with a bunch of yellow flowers. He had a goose-egg in one pocket, and a crooked stick in the other pocket, and some dry cow-manure in his hat. The girl turned up her nose, and when he give her the flowers she threwed them in the firplace. But the big country boy just set down, and grinned like everything was a-going fine. "That fire sure is hot, ain't it?" says he. The girl scowled at him. "My ass is a damn sight hotter," she says.

Pretty near anybody would have been set back when they heard that, but the big country boy just took the egg out of his pocket. "Let's cook my turnip in it, then," says he. The girl looked at him for a minute, and she seen he was different from them common smart-alecks. "How do you figure to get the turnip out, when it's done?" she says. "With this here grab-hook, of course," says the big country boy, and he pulled the crooked stick out of his other pocket. The girl looked at the goose-egg and the crooked stick, and pretty near busted out laughing. But the big country boy was a-leading by two lengths, so she begun to talk nasty. "Oh shit!" she says. "Never mind, here's a plenty," says he, and showed her the hat full of cow-chips.

This time she did bust out laughing sure enough, and so did her father that was a-listening behind the door. The big country boy dropped his cow-shit, and grabbed that girl right where it would do the most good. "By God, she's yours," says the old man, "and a good farm goes with her!" So then all three of them laughed like fools, and the girl knowed the big country boy was just what she wanted. Pretty soon him and her got married, and they lived happy ever after, too.

H507.1

This is clearly a variant of Type 853, in the Aarne-Thompson *Type Index,* and is widely known throughout Europe and North America. In addition to the extensive listings given by Thompson in both the *Type Index* and the *Motif-Index,* it may be found in *Kryptadia,* II, 72–73 (from France) and *Kryptadia,* IV, 344–347 (Belgium). Randolph also makes reference to "History of the Four Rings," Tale III in Robert Hays Cunningham's *Amusing Prose Chap-Books,* pp. 191–193. Although the customary characterization of the girl and her father as princess and king has been lost, and the elements preceding and following the contest of wits between the boy and the girl have been greatly condensed, the basic novella form of the tale persists.

12. Don't Call It Fucking

Told by Bob Wyrick, Eureka Springs, Ark., May 1951. He got it from an old man near Grandview, Ark., in 1907.

One time there was a silly girl that heard about fucking, but she hadn't never done any. She took her old pappy a jug of cider while he was working in the timber. "Pappy," she says, "I want you to fuck me." The old man says, "All right," and cut him a saw-tooth briar. He whipped her ass till she yelled like a steam whistle. So that's what she thought fucking was.

Pretty soon her and one of the neighbor boys got married. The very first night she says, "I never been fucked but once, and I sure don't want no more of it." He asked her who done it, and she says, "My pappy." Next morning the boy went to see pappy, and the old man told him just what happened. "Don't never call it fucking," says pappy. "Just tell her you want to make something for the house, and get her broke in that way." So the boy went to town and got some plates, cups, and saucers. He hid 'em under the bed, and every time they knocked off a chunk he would fetch out a piece of china.

Next time the old man seen the girl he asked her how they are getting along. She says everything is going fine. "I told John the first night that there'd be no fucking," she says. "Me and him spends all our time a-making dishes, and it sure is fun! We've got enough plates, cups and saucers for two families already. And if John don't run out of paste, we're going to make you a fine big piss-pot for Christmas!"

[X731.1.1; X732.2.2]

Randolph suggests that this tale is related to Aarne-Thompson Type 1490*, "The Contract to Be Burned," which, however, lacks the full sequence of the actual whipping by the father and the deception practiced by the husband after marriage. These two essential elements suggest a new type [1491**]. The story is paralleled in *Kryptadia*, IV, 1–7 (Polish Gypsy origin), where the deception practiced is that of baking cakes. Also related is a Russian tale in Afanasiev, *Stories*, p. 34, in which the father dissuades his daughter from accepting a proposal of intercourse by doing it to her with a hot nail. The boy later tells her that his penis is cold, but she feels it and finds it hot.

13. The Man That Had a Baby

Told by George Head, Eureka Springs, Ark., February, 1952.

One time there was a man that thought women always make too much fuss about having a baby. He says it's just natural for a female to shell out young-uns, and don't hurt no more than getting rid of a tape-worm. This crack made the man's wife pretty mad, and she says, "All right, I'll fix it with the doctor so you can have our next baby, and see how you like it." The fellow just laughed, and he says that's fair enough, and we will take turn about from now on.

Next time the fellow got drunk they put him to bed with bandages, and some croton oil for a physic, and the doctor fastened a big stout plaster over his ass-hole. So next morning the man's belly was swelled up like a balloon, and you could hear him hollering all over town. Doc says just take it easy, as these pains will only last four or five hours. Then the fellow begun to kick and raise hell, so it took the whole family to hold him in the bed. Finally the doctor brought a little pet monkey and slipped it under the quilt, and then he cut the big plaster loose. The patient give a whoop and shit all over himself. The bed was plumb full, and running over on the carpet besides. Just then the little monkey showed up, a-wiping hockey out of its eyes, and chattering. Soon as the fellow seen the monkey he begun to holler worse than ever.

"What does the little bastard mean, laughing like a fool when his poor mother is a-dying?" he yelled. Even Doc had to grin when he heard that one, and the man's wife pretty near had a fit.

After Doc left with his monkey, it took the folks all day to clean up the house, and get things a-running orderly again. When the fellow sobered up everybody says he must have dreamed the whole thing, and Doc advised him to go easy on the applejack. The man didn't drink no liquor at all for a long time after that, and he give up talking about how it ain't no trouble for a woman to have a baby.

J2321; [X721.1.1]

Ernest Baughman reported to Randolph that he had heard this tale in Muncie, Indiana, in 1935. In Europe the story is usually told as a joke on a parson or priest; for extensive references, see Aarne-Thompson, *Type Index,* Type 1739, "The Parson and the Calf." Further versions may be found in *Kryptadia,* II, 91–99 (from France), and in Afanasiev, *Stories,* pp. 89–92.

Legman, *Rationale,* I, 600–603, gives a detailed analysis of the theme, including homosexual variants of the story, with references to Hall, *Anecdota,* I, No. 54; *Anecdota,* II, Nos. 46 and 296; and Boccaccio's *Decameron* (Day IX, Tale 3); as well as versions heard in California in 1941 and 1943, and in Florida in 1953.

14. He Didn't Get No Pension

Told by Price Paine, Noel, Mo., October, 1923. He said it was one of many "old soldier jokes" that circulated in McDonald County, Mo., about 1895.

One time there was a fellow named Jubal that fought in the Yank army, but they didn't give him no pension. Jubal says he has got all kinds of ailments, and also he is pretty near blind. Finally the government doctor made Jubal undress and examined him all over, but it looked like he is strong as a horse. There was a card hung up with letters on it, but Jubal says he don't see no letters, and he can't even see the card. They brought a big light to shine in his eyes, but Jubal didn't pay no attention. The government doctor didn't know what to think, but he watched Jubal mighty close.

Pretty soon a girl come in the office, and she pulled up her dress to show her legs. "That sure is a pretty girl, ain't it?" says the doctor. Jubal says he don't see no girl, but he begun to sweat. So then the doctor snapped his finger, and the girl showed a lot more, but Jubal still says he don't see nothing. The doctor made another sign to the girl, and she took off her clothes. There she was, a-prancing around without a stitch on only her shoes and stockings. Jubal never batted an eye, but the girl busted out laughing. "Look at his pecker, Doc," she says. "It's a-standing up like a tree!"

The doctor grinned a little, too. "Your eyesight ain't as bad as you thought it was," says he. Jubal was pretty goddam mad, but he just put on his clothes and walked out of the office. Jubal ain't the only one that was mad, either, because lots of other old soldiers has been done out of their pension the same way. Them government doctors ain't got much sense, but they sure know how to find out if a man is blind or not.

[H249.1]

Randolph notes that there is a similar story in Lockridge, *Waggish Tales*, pp. 47–50. The nexus of the joke is the eyesight test, at first intentionally failed, then passed, literally with "flying colors," against the patient's will. In the broad sense, it belongs to that large group of "soldier jokes," as Randolph's informant puts it, in which the soldier or inductee attempts to fail a crucial part of his induction examination but is caught in his lie by the clever doctor or examining officer. In his chapter on fools (*Rationale*, I, 163), Legman relates a version heard in Orangeburg, N.Y., in 1944; later (p. 244) he presents another, heard on a transcontinental train in 1943. Both, of course, were World War II draftee jokes.

15. The Loss of Jenkin-Horn

Told by Fred High, Berryville, Ark., October, 1953. It was a common story around Green Forest, Ark., about 1910.

One time there was a pretty little girl that lived in the country, and she didn't know much of anything. So then a sheepherder come along, and he showed her his pecker. "What is that thing?" she says, and the boy told her it is called Jenkin-Horn. He was one of these fellows that always wears a buckskin string round his waist for luck, and the girl thought Jenkin-Horn was strapped onto him.

The sheep-herder come around pretty often for awhile, and that girl sure was crazy about Jenkin-Horn. One day the fellow says he is going to live somewheres out West. The girl didn't care if he went or not, but she wanted him to leave Jenkin-Horn for her to play with. They had quite a tussle about it, and when he got on his horse the girl run after him a-hollering for Jenkin-Horn. Well, when they come to the ford a bass happened to jump just then, and she thought Jenkin-Horn had fell in the river. The sheep-herder rode on down the trail, but the girl didn't pay him no mind.

Pretty soon a preacher come along, and he seen her a-crying and splashing around in the water. He asked her what is the matter, and she says Jenkin-Horn is lost. The preacher couldn't make out what the girl meant, but Jenkin-Horn must be something mighty important, so he started to help her hunt for it. Pretty soon the preacher got his pants caught on a sycamore stub. And when the pants tore loose, the girl seen Jenkin-Horn sticking out between the preacher's legs. "There it is!" she hollered. "You old thief, you've got Jenkin-Horn tied on *you!*"

The boys around town used to tell the story for a long time after that. They figured it was a good joke on the preacher, that anybody would think he was trying to steal Jenkin-Horn off of a sheep-herder.

[K1363.5; X712.4.1; X739.1.1]
The Aarne-Thompson *Type Index* lists this as Type 1543A*, "A Combing Machine," with only one version, from Russia, noted. It is also found in *Kryptadia*, II, 1–4 (from France), and Afanasiev, *Stories*, pp. 127–130. The seducer's penis is given a variety of names—combing machine, frenolle, Jenkin Horn—and in some versions the girl later finds it on her father rather than on the parson. Legman, *Rationale*, I, 552, discusses "horn" as a symbol for the penis. In connection with the preacher's role in the tale, Randolph makes reference to Parsons, *Folk Tales of the Antilles*, p. 325, "Why Priests Wear Drawers."

16. It Didn't Cost Him Nothing

Told by Fred High, Berryville, Ark., October, 1953. He heard it near Green Forest, Ark., about 1900.

One time a man and his wife come a-walking down the road, and their pretty daughter was with them. Two boys from Green Forest rode up, and one of 'em says to the other, "I bet you five dollars I can screw that girl, right before her folks, and not cost me a cent." The other fellow says, "It's a bet." Then the young fellow hollered to the girl's father, "I bet five dollars I can lift all three of you, if you will lay still like I say." The old man figured it can't be done, so he pulled out a five-dollar bill.

Well, the young fellow told the girl's father to lay flat down in the road. The woman laid on her husband, and that put the pretty girl on top. The Green Forest boy took down his pants and went at it, but the girl begun to kick. "You got to lay still like I tell you," says the young fellow, "because that is part of the bet." The old man was on the bottom of the pile, so he couldn't see what was going on. "Lay still, daughter," says he, "that's the last five dollars we got." So the pretty girl done what her pappy said, and the young fellow sure give her a good fucking.

Soon as he got his pants buttoned up, the fellow says, "Well, you folks are heavier than I thought, so I lose the bet," and he give the old man five dollars. But he won the first bet all right, so the other fellow had to give him five dollars. The way it turned out, the boy from Green Forest just broke even, and he got to screw the pretty girl for nothing.

The girl just grinned when she seen how things was, but the other fellow grumbled a good deal. There wasn't nothing to do about it, though, because he lost the bet fair and square. It just goes to show that a smart young fellow can get pretty near anything he wants in this world, if he knows how to go after it.

[X724.1.2]

A more widespread form of this tale omits the element of the wager and focuses on the youth's quick-wittedness in deceptively gaining the man's assent to intercourse with his daughter (sometimes two daughters), wife, or both. See the references in Aarne-Thompson, *Type Index,* under Type 1563, "Both?" Other versions may be found in *Kryptadia,* IV, 338–340 (from Belgium), and Afanasiev, *Stories,* pp. 106–108, 112–115, 118–120, as well as in Randolph's *The Devil's Pretty Daughter,* pp. 78–79.

The element of the wager enters into still another form of the tale, in *Kryptadia,* II, 163–164 (France). In this form, the wager is between a servant and his mistress; he may have his will of her if he can lie naked in bed with her for one hour without having an erection. He ties his penis down, but the string breaks and he apparently loses the wager. However, the case is taken to court, and through clever hyperbole the servant wins.

17. The Two Preachers

Told by Jeff Strong, at Roaring River near Cassville, Mo., April, 1941. He got it from "Watermelon Charley" Smith, of Aurora, Mo. I have heard several versions of this tale.

One time there was two preachers holding a big camp-meeting out in the woods. The big fellow was just a young squirt, but the other preacher was pretty old. They was both married, but they done a lot of outside fucking on camp-meeting nights. So one evening they got to bragging how many of the womenfolks they had diddled. And that same night they both stood in front of the brush-arbor while the congregation was a-coming in.

Whenever a woman came along that one of 'em had screwed, he would say "Amen!" And if a woman come past that both of 'em had laid up with, they would both holler "Amen!" It was surprising how many of the womenfolks them two preachers had got next to. Both of 'em kept hollering "Amen" like it was some kind of a game, and they was having a lot of fun out of it.

Pretty soon the young preacher's wife come along, so naturally he hollered "Amen!" but so did the other fellow. The young preacher scowled something terrible, but he couldn't do nothing about it right then. So they just stood there, and it wasn't long till the old preacher's wife showed up with her daughter, that was just a teen-age girl. The old preacher says "Amen!" when her and the girl come by. But the young preacher says "Amen! Amen!" like that.

The old man just stood there with his mouth open for a minute, and then him and the young fellow begun to fight like a couple of wildcats. Some of the menfolks run out and pulled 'em apart, but the revival was plumb ruined. Everybody says it is a terrible disgrace for ministers of the gospel to act like that, right in front of a church house. But the folks that live around there never did find out what them preachers was a-fighting about.

K1541

The Aarne-Thompson *Type Index* notes this as Type 1781, "Sexton's Own Wife Brings Her Offering," and traces it as far back as the early sixteenth-century *Facetiae* of Heinrich Bebel, as well as noting it in Finnish tradition. Randolph notes a text from Oklahoma in Mitchell, *The Wing and the Yoke,* p. 66. Abrahams, *Deep Down in the Jungle,* pp. 199–200, relates a version from a black informant in Philadelphia. A variant form, in which the members of the clergy are replaced by a doctor and a lawyer, who argue about which profession provides the greater opportunity to seduce clients, is given by Legman in *Rationale,* I, 757–758; it was heard in Minneapolis in 1935.

18. Collins and the Doctor

Told by Oakley St. John, Pineville, Mo., July, 1921. He related it as the experience of a physician at Anderson, Mo., about 1910.

One time there was a young fellow named Collins, that didn't have much sense. Collins was always a-laying up with them girls on South Mountain, so pretty soon he got the clap. We all seen him go tearing into Doc Holton's office that morning, and there was several people a-waiting, but Collins didn't pay them no mind. "Oh, Doc," says he, "there's something wrong with my prick—" but just then Doc pulled the damn fool into the office, and told him not to talk like that no more. "If you've got to holler," says Doc, "call it your arm." He give Collins some clap-medicine, and told him to come back Saturday morning.

Well, the office was plumb full of folks on Saturday, and there was lots of women amongst them. Doc seen Collins a-coming this time, so he sung out, "How's your arm this morning?" Collins drawed a deep breath. "Swole plumb to a strut, Doc," says he. "So goddam sore I can't hardly piss though it."

Them people in the waiting-room just set there with their mouth open, and Doc couldn't help but bust out laughing. There was two or three old sisters walked out of the office, but Doc didn't say a word about Collins's language. If a fellow ain't got no more sense than that, it ain't much use trying to tell him anything.

[X712.5.1]
Ernest Baughman informed Randolph that he had heard this story in Bloomington, Ind., about 1945. Legman, *Rationale*, I, 155, reports it from Washington, D.C., in 1949. He also notes a variant form (p. 63), again from Washington, in 1950. A boy is told by his mother to say "whisper" instead of "piss"; however, the father is not informed of the code, and when the boy says he wants to "whisper," the father invites him to do it in his ear.

Still another variant may be found in Hall, *Anecdota*, II, No. 17, in which the mother instructs her little girl to wave her hand in front of her face instead of saying "pee-pee." The next day, before assembled company, the girl waves her hand, and the mother tells her that she understands and to run along. The daughter, still waving, adds, "And shit!" The joke, of course, in all instances hinges on the misuse, misunderstanding, or inadequacy of euphemisms for urination, generally combined with the ingenuousness of a child or a not very bright adult whose impulse is to express himself directly.

19. The Rabbit Got 'Em Told

Told by Miss Virginia Tyler, Eureka Springs, Ark., August, 1953.

One time there was a turtle, a lizard, and a rabbit lived together in Arkansas. It was a bad year, so they put their stuff in a handcart and moved to Oklahoma. Soon as the shanty was built they planted a little garden, but the truck wouldn't grow because there wasn't no fertilizer. Finally they cut the cards, and the rabbit was low man. So next morning he took the handcart and started back to Arkansas, after a load of manure.

Right after he left they struck oil in Oklahoma, but the rabbit didn't hear nothing about it. When he finally got back, the shanty was gone. The folks had a new house, and there was fine lawns, and a swimming pool, and a big oil well in the pasture. The rabbit knocked on the door, and out came a servant with brass buttons on his coat. "Is old Turtle here?" The servant sniffed when he seen the cart full of manure. "Mister Tour*telle* is out at the well," says he. The rabbit scowled, and then he says, "Where's old Lizard?" The man just stared at him for a minute. "Mister Liz*zarde* is out in the yard," says the servant.

The rabbit just stood there on the porch for a minute, looking around at all them fine things. "Well," says he, "you tell them son-of-a-bitches that Mister Rab*bitt* is here with the—fertilizer!"

[X716.3.1]

Ernest Baughman reported to Randolph that he had heard this in Indiana, with "shit" instead of "fertilizer" for the last word. That, of course, is the form in which it should be told, for the point of the joke is to destroy the pretentiousness of the servant with the use of what is ordinarily a taboo word. The use of the word "fertilizer" by Randolph's informant carries an element of sarcasm, but it weakens the impact of the punch line. Legman, *Rationale*, II, 683, gives the story as heard from a soldier in Washington, D.C., in 1949. Richard Buehler, for his master's thesis on obscene humor at the Bloomington campus of Indiana University collected the story from a Mooresville, Ind., girl. Abrahams, *Deep Down in the Jungle*, pp. 247–248, reports it from black tradition in Philadelphia. In all three instances the last line is delivered with the word "shit."

20. A Long Time Back

Told by Carl Withers, New York, October, 1948. He heard it in Hickory County, Mo., about 1940.

One time there was two old men got to arguing about how far back they could remember. Both of 'em knowed what happened when they was six months old, also things that took place when they was three months old. Them fellows remembered cutting their baby teeth, and even the first time they ever tasted milk. It wasn't no trouble to recollect what their own afterbirth looked like, neither, when they got to going good.

Finally one fellow says that several weeks before he was born his mother was setting out cabbage plants, and she had to straddle the row. "Just for a joke," he says, "I used to reach out and pull them plants up, faster than Maw could set 'em. I was a mean little devil in them days."

The other fellow looked kind of bothered for a minute, and then he remembered the time his pappy was screwing an Osage girl, and it must have been about ten months before he was born. "It was my turn to be shot," says he, "but I just reached up and grabbed my young brother by the legs, to keep from going into the squaw's twitchet. That's how close I come to being a goddam Indian," he says.

The first old man just set there with his mouth open, and he didn't have no more to say. But the whole thing is kind of mixed up, and maybe part of it ain't true, anyhow. When all's said and done, it's hard to tell which one of them fellows could remember the farthest back.

[X721.2.1]

Baughman, in his *Type and Motif-Index of the Folktales of England and North America,* assigns this the motif number X1014.1*, under the heading of "Lie: Remarkable Memory." His tale source, Donald Day, *Publications of the Texas Folklore Society,* XIX (1944), 69, is a "cleaned up" version of the story, and the emphasis must be on the big lie. In Randolph's version the lie, of course, is present, but the stronger emphasis is on the element of sexual humor. Legman, *Rationale,* I, 586, relates a version similar to Randolph's, heard in New York in 1947, with a maid in place of the Indian squaw.

21. The Half-Wit and the Eel

Told by Fred High, Berryville, Ark., October, 1953. He heard it near Berryville in the 1890's.

One time a rich man's daughter got to playing with a live eel, and she lost it in her. The whole family was scared pretty bad, and they called the doctor, but his forceps was too short.

Finally the doctor says they had better get some long-peckered fellow to fuck her, so the eel would grab hold of his prick and be drug out that way.

The family was very anxious to keep down scandal, so they got a big half-wit boy from way out in the country. The folks figured that if he was to tell anybody, they wouldn't believe it on account of him being a half-wit. The rich man give the fellow ten dollars to screw his daughter, but of course he didn't say nothing about the eel.

The half-wit went in the girl's room, while the rich man waited outside. Pretty soon he could hear the bed a-squeaking. All of a sudden there was two or three loud yells. Here come the half-wit a-tearing out, with a big old eel a-hanging onto his pecker. So then he run for the river, a-hollering at the top of his voice. The rich man says all's well that ends well, and we will forget the whole business. But for God's sake don't put no more eels up your twitchet, he says.

It was a long time after that, when somebody in the tavern happened to mention the rich man's daughter. The big half-wit was a-setting there, and he says "I screwed that girl one time." The boys all winked at each other behind his back, and one of 'em says, "Was it any good?" The half-wit looked mighty solemn, and shook his head. "No," he says, "her ass was full of blacksnakes." Them fool boys all laughed like hell, because everybody thought he was crazy as a bedbug. They didn't have no idea how close that half-wit come to telling the truth.

[X712.1.2.1]
Another version of this tale may be found in *Kryptadia*, IV, 315–318 (from Belgium). All the tale and joke versions belong to the large family of "vagina dentata" stories. A variant form of the tale, that of seduction under the guise of retrieving lost objects from the vagina, goes at least as far back as the fifteenth-

century *One Hundred Merrie and Delightsome Stories* (ed. de la Sale), No. 3, "The Search for the Ring."

In *Rationale*, II, 429–430, Legman notes a French version published in 1929, also with an eel, turned specifically into a joke with a punch line. He further points out a Korean joke published in 1962, in which a mouse runs into a woman's vagina and later bites her lover's penis.

A 1971 X-rated motion picture, "The Nurses," uses the variant form of the theme, the recovery of lost objects. During his examination of a woman patient, a doctor discovers that she has pushed various objects into her vagina. After removing a couple of them with his fingers, he states that he needs a longer tool for the rest, whereupon he drops his trousers and mounts her.

22. Cut Their Knockers Off!

Told by Fred High, Berryville, Ark., October, 1953. It was a common story, he says, along the Arkansas-Oklahoma border in the 1890's.

One time a fellow had a wife that was a lot younger than him, and she got to fooling with other men. So he sold the farm and moved a long way off, to get a new start where the people was all strangers. He told his wife that the folks in this part of the country didn't do no fucking, because every man for miles around was cut like a steer. And he told the neighbors that his wife has been in the lunatic asylum because she carried a little sharp knife, and would whack a man's knockers off every time she got a chance.

So that was why the menfolks kept away from the newcomer's wife, but the woman didn't care because she thought they was all geldings anyhow. But finally she got to thinking that maybe some of the young fellows has not been dehorned yet. They had a hired man that was only fifteen years old, but big and stout for his age. One night the woman went down to the shed-room where the hired man slept, and she slipped into the bed with him.

The boy kind of waked up and grabbed her, before he rightly knowed who it was. But the moonlight come in the window, and he seen her face. And just then the woman put her hand under the blanket, to feel whether he was cut like a steer. Soon as she done that, the young fellow was scared pretty near to death, and he jumped out of the bed. "I've heard about you!" he says. "Nobody is going to whack *my* balls off!"

The woman says for God's sake shut up, but the boy wouldn't stay in the house another minute. He run right down the road in his shirt-tail, and told it all over the neighborhood how the crazy woman tried to cut his knockers off. She had a hard time after that, because no man in the whole country would let her come within ten foot of him. So finally the poor woman just kind of give up, and got along with her old husband the best she could.

[X714.1.1]
Ernest Baughman suggested to Randolph that this is somewhat related to Aarne-Thompson Type 1381, in talkative aspect only. More properly, it belongs to the complex of tales under Type 1359 and Motif K1569, "The Husband Outwits Adulteress and Paramour," in several forms of which the husband castrates or threatens to castrate the wife's would-be lover. In Randolph's tale the castratory threat is made to come from the wife, but it is the clever husband who originates it.

23. The New Hired Man

Told by Bob Wyrick, Eureka Springs, Ark., March, 1950. He heard it near Green Forest, Ark., about 1900.

One time there was a young fellow come a-walking down the road, and it looked like he was about sixteen years old. He asked the farmer to hire him, and just then a bull topped a cow right by the barn. "What's that animal a-doing?" says the farmer, and the boy answered, "I reckon he's just a-r'aring up to see the grass." When the farmer heard that he says, "You are just the man I am looking for, because most of the farmhands talk so rough I won't have 'em in my house." So then he wants to know what the young man's name is, and the fellow says, "Just call me Fuckemboth."

When they got to the house the farmer says, "This is my daughter Nelly, and this is my wife." And then he pulled up Nelly's dress to show her cunt, and he says, "That is the jail house." Next he pulled up his wife's dress to show her cunt, and he says, "That is the penitentiary." He give the fellow a hard look. "Them is two places a young man better keep away from," says he. And then the farmer walked out of the house.

Nelly and the old woman stood there a-looking at the young fellow. "So you are the new hired man," says Nelly, and then she wants to know what his name is. "Just call me Beans," says the boy. Nelly kind of giggled, and she says it's a funny name, but easy to remember. And the old woman says that reminds me, we have got beans in the pot right now. The farmer come back in the house then, and they all set down and eat their supper.

Pretty soon they went to bed, and it was not a very big house. Along in the night Nelly begun to grunt and fart pretty loud. The farmer roused up, and he says "Nelly, what's the matter?" The girl drawed a deep breath. "Beans is laying heavy on my stomach," she says, and the old man went back to sleep. After while Nelly begun to grunt and fart again, so the old woman got up and went over to see about it. She seen that Beans was laying on her daughter sure enough, and she begun to holler for the old man. The farmer was about half asleep, and he didn't understand all this hollering about beans. All of a sudden he thought of the new hired man, so he sung out "Fuckemboth! Fuckemboth!" The boy didn't return no answer, but the old woman sure was surprised to hear her husband a-talking like that. She just went back to bed, and never said another word. The farmer dropped off to sleep again, and the new hired man went right ahead with what he was a-doing.

When they got up next morning the young fellow walked over to the fireplace, with his pecker a-sticking out so you could have hung your hat on it. "Looks like a night in jail didn't do no good," says Nelly. The old woman just kind of giggled. "If he don't quieten down, I reckon we'll have to put him in the penitentiary," she says. The hired man didn't return no answer, but pretty soon he quit his job and walked on down the road. A young fellow don't mind going to jail once in a while, but the penitentiary is something else again.

K1327; K1399.2

This tale is a combination of Aarne-Thompson Types 1545, "The Boy with Many Names," and 1545B, "The Boy Who Knew Nothing of Women," and is related as well to Type 1563, "Both?" In these various forms, Thompson lists versions from throughout Europe and North America. Further versions may be found in *Kryptadia*, II, 59–60, 61–62, 117–119, 119–121 (from France); IV, 348–352 (Belgium); Afanasiev, *Stories*, pp. 94–96; and from black tradition in Philadelphia, in Abrahams, *Deep Down in the Jungle*, pp. 250–251. Afanasiev's is actually a variant form, focusing on a wager between the priest and his servant as to who will be the first to use indecent language. The servant wins when he mounts the priest's wife and daughter, whose vulvas the priest, like Randolph's farmer, has identified by "prison" terminology.

24. It Was Hell, All Right

Told by J. L. Russell, Harrison, Ark., April, 1950. He heard it in Carroll County, Ark., in the late 1880's.

One time there was a wicked man that died and went to Hell. But when he got there, it looked like a big park. There was fine blue-grass lawns, and fountains, and benches for folks to set on, and flowers a-blooming, and pretty girls a-walking up and down. "It ain't what I expected," says the wicked man. "Why, this is one of the prettiest places I ever seen."

He set down on a nice bench in the shade, and thought about it. Pretty soon the idea come in his mind that maybe he got into Heaven accidental, because some book-keeper has made a mistake. "I better lay low and sing small," says the wicked man, "or else whoever runs things here is liable to throw me out." He kept quiet for a long time, till a fat Yankee set down on the same bench. And then the wicked man says, "Mister, what is the name of this here settlement?" The fellow just looked at him. "You must be a newcomer," says the Yankee. "This is Hell, and you're a-setting right in the middle of it."

The wicked man looked around, and seen how fine everything was. "I don't believe it," he says. "Maybe not," says the fat Yankee, "but this is Hell, all right. You'll find out soon enough." Just then some pretty girls come along, with dresses clear up to their ass like they wear at Hot Springs. So the wicked man bantered one of 'em to go behind some bushes with him. In about two minutes he come a-tearing out, and dragged another girl into the bushes. Then he come running back after the third one, but she didn't suit him, neither.

The fat Yankee was still a-setting on the bench, and the wicked man flopped down beside him. "Goddam it, the girls here ain't got no cunts!" says he. The Yankee just wagged his silly head. "Yeah, I thought you would find out," he says.

[Q569.6]
Ernest Baughman reported the tale to Randolph from Albuquerque in 1950. Hall, *Anecdota,* II, No. 392, gives a version naming Frank Harris as the victim. In *Rationale,* I, 389, Legman relates a version collected in Washington, D.C., in 1943, in which Hell is described as clouds floating by with barrels of beer and girls on them—the barrels have holes in them, the girls don't. Buehler in his master's thesis (pp. 19–21) gives a variant from a New York informant which omits the setting in Hell. A man seduces a beautiful girl only to find that she has no vagina between her legs. He is convulsed with laughter at the sight, and in retaliation she threatens to piss on him, raising her arm and baring an unshaved armpit.

The theme of sexual frustration in Hell has been explored by Sartre in his play, "No Exit"; Garcin finds Hell to be a drawing room which he must share with two women, Estelle and Inez, who symbolically have no vaginas. The 1972 X-rated motion picture, "The Devil in Miss Jones," reverses the situation; in Hell, the sexually possessed Miss Jones is confined in a room with a man who symbolically has no penis.

25. She Knowed What She Wanted

Told by Bob Wyrick, Eureka Springs, Ark., March, 1950. He heard it near Green Forest, Ark., in 1917.

One time there was a widow woman had a pretty daughter, and three young fellows come a-sparking. All of a sudden a big storm blowed up, so the widow woman says they better stay all night. The three men took the big bed, and the girl slept with her mother behind the partition. Along in the night them three fellows got to talking, and the womenfolks could hear every word they said.

The first man begun to tell how many steers he owned, and the price of beef is going up every day, so he will be very rich. The widow woman nudged her daughter. "Listen, Betty," she whispered, "that's the man for you."

The second fellow says they have struck oil on his land in Oklahoma, so now he's got more money than Carter had oats. The widow woman nudged her daughter. "Listen, Betty," she whispered, "that's the man for you."

After while the third boy spoke up. "Move over, will you?" says he. "Both of you fellows is laying on my prick." The girl nudged her mother. "Listen, Maw," she whispered, "*that's* the man for me!"

So next day her and the long-peckered boy got married, and that's all there is to the story. It just goes to show that Betty knowed what she wanted, anyhow. Which is more than lots of old folks can say nowadays.

[F547.3.1.1]

The same story may be found in Hall, *Anecdota*, II, No. 282, in a somewhat condensed, more specifically joke form. Legman, *Rationale*, I, 328, gives it as heard in Washington, D.C., in 1944, in a Chinese context and with a punning conclusion. Two Chinese girls brag of the wealth of their mandarin lovers, symbolized by dragons on their doors. The third states that her lover has one dragon, but that one draggin' on the ground. He also notes a version collected in California in 1940, with the context rationalized to Marines who have dragons tattooed on their chests.

26. Bud Claypool Couldn't Spell

Told by J. L. Russell, Harrison, Ark., April, 1950. He heard it in Carroll County, Ark., about 1890.

One time a young lawyer named Bud Claypool was a-running for Congress, so he stumped the whole district, and made speeches all over the country. Us home folks figured that Bud was a pretty good man, and it looked like he might be elected. But here come a farmer from Buffalo River that was a-talking mighty strong against him.

"Why, gentlemen," says the farmer, "that young jackleg ain't no good! Surely you ain't going to send him to represent us in Washington! It's fellows like Bud Claypool that has give Arkansas a bad name!"

The people that hung around the county seat couldn't make out what the old farmer was up to. "It looks to me like Bud is a pretty smart lawyer," says one of them courthouse rats. "What's the matter with him, anyhow?"

The old man scowled at the crowd. "The damn fool ain't got no book-learning," says he. "Everybody knows that a congressman ought to be educated. But this here Claypool can't write a common everyday letter, without it is full of mistakes."

Some of the boys got to arguing with the old man, just for the hell of it. "How do you know Bud can't write?" says one. "Did you ever correspond with him?"

The old farmer scowled worse than ever. "No, the son-of-a-bitch never wrote to me," he says. "But my daughter got several letters from him, and I examined 'em careful. Gentlemen, a fellow that spells CUNT with a K ain't got no business in the Congress of the United States!"

Them boys hollered so loud you could hear 'em clear to the crossroads, and the old farmer just got in his wagon and went home. The story got around, of course, and people all over the district was laughing about it. Bud Claypool lost the election, and some folks thought the old farmer from Buffalo River was the cause of it. But maybe Bud would have got beat anyhow. You can't never tell about things like that.

[X749.2.1]
Although this story is a local anecdote, the spelling of "cunt" with a "k" occurs regularly in humorous erotica. In *The Limerick,* Legman gives two examples of that verse form (Nos. 914 and 1379) concerned with such a misspelling. The first originally appeared in [T. R. Smith, ed.?], *Immortalia,* a 1927 American volume of erotic verse, and the second in *The Pearl,* an English erotic periodical of 1879–81. In *Rationale,* I, 154, Legman also relates a joke, collected in Fredericksburg, Va., in 1952, in which a group of men debate on what is the most beautiful part of a woman, and one observes that certain people spell it with a "k."

27. Old Age in Arkansas

Told by Gene Carter, Eureka Springs, Ark., September, 1953. He had it from Harry Wilks, also of Eureka Springs, in 1949.

One time there was a fellow lived in Illinois, and he heard a lot of wild stories about Arkansas. So finally he come down here to see about it. The people in Fayetteville and Little Rock acted just about like the folks he knowed back home, and it was kind of a disappointment. He was a-looking for barefooted hillbillies, with coonskin caps on. Somebody told him to leave his car in Durgonville, and foller the river road a-foot, so that's what he done.

The first thing he seen was some young folks a-fucking under the trees. But he didn't pay no attention to that, because the boys and girls in Chicago does the same thing, and think nothing of it.

Pretty soon he come to a log house, and one of the boys had ketched a live jackrabbit. So the boy was a-diddling the rabbit, right there in the front yard. The fellow stopped and watched the boy for quite a while, because he never seen nothing like that back home. They don't have no jackrabbits in Chicago.

After while he walked on down the road, and there was an old man with a long white beard. The old man set on a rail fence, and he was a-playing with his pecker. The fellow spoke the time of day, and the old man says howdy polite enough, but he went right ahead with what he was a-doing. The city fellow stopped and watched the old man for quite a while, because he never seen nothing like that back home.

"Well, by God!" says he. "Maybe it's all true, them stories they tell about Arkansas!" The old man kind of slowed up for a minute, and he says, "What's wrong with Arkansas, stranger?" The fellow told how he seen a boy screwing a rabbit, and now here's an old gentleman with white whiskers a-playing with his pecker. "It looks kind of funny to me," he says. The old man just stared at him. "What's funny about it?" says he. "You can't expect me, at my time of life, to ketch jackrabbits like them young fellows."

[X737.1]
There are two levels of humor in this story. The obvious joke level is carried through by the punch line, in which the old man blandly tells the stranger that of course he must play with himself, since he is too old to catch and screw jackrabbits. More subtle is the local anecdote levels, indirectly poking fun at the outsider who visits Arkansas to check on the truth of the wild stories he has heard about it. Randolph's volume, *We Always Lie to Strangers*, is largely devoted to more polite examples of the same kind of leg-pulling humor.

45

28. The Sailor's Language

Told by Miss Virginia Tyler, Eureka Springs, Ark., November, 1953.

One time there was a country boy that had joined the Navy, and he went a-swaggering around Little Rock. He looked pretty good in his uniform with the ribbons on it, and lots of people was a-buying him drinks. The boy got uncommon drunk, because he was not used to store-boughten liquor. A pretty girl says, "Hello, sailor," and so they went up to her room in the hotel.

The pretty girl wanted her money before they done anything serious, and he give her two dollars. The sailor figured he was getting on fine, but the truth is he had drunk too much for that kind of business. After while he says, "How am I doin', Babe?" The pretty girl just kind of yawned, and she says, "Oh, about three knots."

Well, what she said is Navy talk, all right. But the sailor was kind of bothered. "What do you mean, three knots?" says he. The girl just yawned again. "Well," she says, "it's not hard, and it's not in, and you're not going to get your two dollars back."

[X735.5.1]
I have been unable to find any parallels to this punning story. In the broad sense, it is related to Number 67 of this collection, "Let's Play Whammy," in the backfiring of intended sexual performance under the influence of alcohol.

29. Fill, Bowl, Fill

Told by Lew Swigart, Lamar, Mo., June, 1927. He has one version for men only, and another for mixed audiences. I printed the latter in Who Blowed Up the Church House *(1952, pp. 17–19, 185–186) with annotations by Herbert Halpert.*

One time there was a king that had a pretty daughter. Their hired man's name was Jimmy, and he got to fooling with the princess, so the king seen something would have to be done about it. They had a pet rabbit that always come to the king's house at night, and the rule was that if Jimmy kept the rabbit for a week he could marry the king's daughter. Jimmy took it over to where he lived, and trained the rabbit so it would come when he rung a bell.

The king promised the servant girl if she would fetch the rabbit he'd give her five pounds, as money went by the pound in them days. She told Jimmy she would give him half if he would let her have the rabbit. "No," says Jimmy, "I won't do it. But if you will lay down and let me hone you off, you can have the rabbit." So he laid her down and honed her off. She picked up the rabbit and started home to the king's house, but Jimmy rung the bell, and the rabbit broke loose and come back. So she went home and told the king she couldn't get the rabbit.

Well, the king promised his daughter if she would fetch the rabbit he'd give her two hundred pounds. She went over and says to Jimmy, "We are going to get married anyhow, and two hundred pounds would be nice for us to have." But Jimmy says he don't want no money. "If you will lay down and let me hone you off, you can have the rabbit," says he. So he laid her down and honed her off. She picked up the rabbit and started home for the king's house, but Jimmy rung the bell, and the rabbit broke loose and come back. So she went home and told the king she couldn't get the rabbit.

Next the king promised his wife if she would fetch the rabbit he'd give her three hundred pounds. She went over and told Jimmy she would give him half the money if he would let her have the rabbit. "I'll give you a little more than half," she says. "No," says Jimmy, "but if you will lay down and let me hone you off you can have the rabbit." So he laid her down and honed her off. She picked up the rabbit and started home for the king's house, but Jimmy rung the bell, and the rabbit broke loose and come back. So she went home and told the king she couldn't get the rabbit.

Late in the night here come the king himself, and says he will give five hundred pounds for the rabbit. "Hell no," says Jimmy. "But there stands my old jenny. I will back her up to the fence, and if you hone her off you can have the rabbit." So he unhitched the old jenny from the cart, and the king honed her off. He picked up the rabbit and told Jimmy to come home with him. When they got to the king's house there was a big bowl setting in the middle of the floor. The king says, "Jimmy, are you a good singer?" and Jimmy allowed he was pretty good. "Well," says the king, "if you can sing that bowl full, you can marry my daughter. But if you don't sing it full, I am going to cut your pecker off." So Jimmy done the best he could, and this is what he sung:

honed her off, Fill, bowl, fill!

The next come over was the king's own daughter
To steal away my skill,
I laid her down and honed her off,
Fill, bowl, fill!

The next come over was the king's own wife
To steal away my skill,
I laid her down and honed her off,
Fill, bowl, fill!

The last to come was the king himself
To steal away my skill,
I backed old Jenny up to the fence
And . . .

"Hold on, Jimmy," says the king. "Don't sing another word. The bowl's plumb full, and you can have my daughter!"

H1112; [D1441.3; M224; K1358.2]; H1045; L161

In his excellent annotations to the polite version of this *cante fable*, Herbert Halpert makes reference to both American and British parallels, and indicates that it is a form of Aarne-Thompson Type 570, "The Rabbit Herd." It is not unique to the Ozarks in this bawdy form either, and I have suggested the creation of a new Type, 570B. A version from France, in *Kryptadia*, II, 45-53, has the boy recall the rabbit with a magic stick, and, in anticipation of his final test, collected three pieces of skin: from a nobleman's hand, the princess' maidenhead, and the king's backside. A somewhat shorter variant in Afanasiev, *Stories*, pp. 169-172, has the serf controlling a herd of hares with a magic whistle and baffling efforts to steal one of them by his master and mistress. Omitted from both Randolph's and Afanasiev's tales, but present in the French version, is the customary element of the three competing brothers, with success going to the youngest.

30. The Romping Party

Told by J. L. Russell, Harrison, Ark., April, 1950. He had it from some boys near Berryville, Ark., in the early 1890's.

One time the old folks was called away unexpected, and their three daughters was all alone in the house. So they got two of the neighbor girls to stay all night with them. After supper they played games awhile, and then just set around talking about boys. Finally the biggest girl blowed out the lights, and she says this is our chance to have a romping party.

Them girls all stripped off naked, and then they got to playing with bananas. It wasn't no real bananas, but just wax imitations out of the big glass dish in the parlor. Country girls always get kind of noisy when they are a-romping in the dark, and a neighbor boy sneaked up to see what was going on. When he found out how things was, that fellow just took off his clothes and slipped in amongst the girls. Then he grabbed the biggest one and give her a real fucking. She squealed and farted like a mare, and then just laid still awhile. The boy sneaked out the door again, and nobody knowed he'd been there at all.

The biggest girl was still a-breathing hard, but pretty soon she begun to holler. "Mamie," she says, "come back here with that *good* banana!" Poor Mamie and the others done the best they could, but the biggest girl kept a-grumbling, as she claimed somebody is holding out on her. There was considerable talk about it, with everybody getting mad, so the neighbor girls just put on their clothes and went home.

Along about fodder-pulling time the biggest girl married one of them spindle-assed Pritchett boys, and they moved into town. She never took no interest in romping parties after that. Her mother-in-law says such things are foolish, and maybe sinful besides.

[X735.3.2]

Legman, *Rationale*, I, 364–365, suggests that this is related to the group of tales in which pregnancy results after women have used candles as dildoes. He notes two forms of the story: that in which nuns become pregnant after using candles made of sperm oil into which sailors had masturbated while at sea (Hall, *Anecdota*, II, No. 295, and heard in Scranton, Penna., in 1925); and, more closely paralleling Randolph's tale, that in which a man in disguise has been smuggled into a party of women, originating in the Italian *novelieri*, as well as collected in Idaho in 1932.

A 1920's American stag film, "Chinese Love Life," uses the theme of a man smuggled in with two girls who are in the habit of engaging in sexual play with each other. And in many stag films bananas are used as substitute penises in onanistic activity among girls, ranking second only to candles for that function.

31. Seminole Medicine

Told by Bob Duncan, Oklahoma City, Okla., September, 1950. He credits it to Ebon Ryan, who worked at Seminole City in the 1920's.

One time there was a boy got his leg broke, and two other fellows stuck around while somebody rode after the doctor. The whiskey was all gone, but they give the patient some Seminole medicine to cheer him up. "Do you know how they make that stuff?" says one. "Sure I do," the other man says, "you just mix grain alcohol and horse piss, with a chaw of tobacco for flavor."

The first fellow just nodded his head. "That's right," says he, "and it's the best tonic in the Territory. My little brother was weak as a cat, but we give him that Seminole remedy for six days, and it sure fixed him up. He walked into the pool-hall Saturday night, and smashed two balls together. Didn't leave nothing but a little pile of dust."

"Yeah, that's how it works," says the other fellow. "My brother-in-law got so puny, the hens thought he was a worm. But Sis fed him that medicine, and he sure mended fast. He whipped everybody on the place, and then grabbed our two big bulls, and swung 'em round his head. When they come together it shook the whole township, like a earthquake."

"What become of the critters?" asked the first man.

"We never did rightly know what went with them bulls," the other fellow answered. "There wasn't nothing left only a big pile of bull-shit."

Neither one of them story-tellers cracked a smile, but the boy on the ground laughed so hard that he forgot all about his leg. He was still a-laughing when the doctor come and took him off to the hospital.

[X1870]

Randolph notes a slightly different text in Duncan's *The Dicky Bird Was Singing*, pp. 126–127. He also mentions having heard, in Pineville, Mo., in 1927, of a man who smashed apples together to produce applesauce, a second man who slammed bricks together to produce brick dust, and a third who tried it with bulls and got bull shit. Ernest Baughman reported having heard this in Indiana about 1925. The story, of course, is a lying contest. Aarne-Thompson, *Type Index,* presents a long list of variants under Type 1920, "Contest in Lying," as well as more than a dozen related sub-types.

32. The Dutch Doctor

Told by Carl Withers, New York, October, 1948. He got it from a farmer in Hickory County, Mo., about 1940.

One time there was a Dutch doctor in this town that could cure anybody, and it didn't make no difference what was the matter with them. A fellow come walking in that day, and he says, "Doc, I have got three bad ailments." So the doctor says for him to speak right up, because everything is going to be all right.

"Well," says the fellow, "I can't taste nothing, and I can't tell the truth about anything, and my memory has failed besides." The doctor studied awhile, and then he went out to the privy and filled two big capsules with fresh hockey. "Chaw up one of them capsules right now," he says, and so the fellow done it. "What does that medicine taste like?" says the doctor. The fellow made a bad face, and he says it tastes like shit.

"That's fine!" says the Dutch doctor. "You can taste all right now, and you can tell the truth as good as anybody. The next time you can't remember something, just chaw up the other capsule!" So then Doc made the fellow give him two dollars, and that is the end of the story.

[J1115.2.3]
The Aarne-Thompson *Type Index* notes a single version of this tale, from Lithuania, under Type 1543C*, "The Clever Doctor." The only difference in the symptoms given by the patients is the substitution of the sense of taste for the sense of smell.

33. Let's Trade Twitchets

Told by Mrs. Mary Alice Blake, Monett, Mo., July, 1946.
She heard it in Christian County, Mo., about 1940.

One time there was a fellow from Springfield come down to the James River, and some peckerwoods was having a square dance. Most of them was drinking out of fruit-jars, and it looked like they was kind of a wild bunch. Soon as a set was over the fiddlers would play a few bars of "Old Horny," and then every man grabbed a girl and took her out in the brush.

Pretty soon the city fellow begun to feel his cork a-bobbing, so the next time "Old Horny" come around he picked out a likely-looking girl. When they got to the brush he says, "Are you married?" and the girl answered, "Nope." Then he says, "Do you want to do a little fucking?" and the girl answered, "Yep." So she hoisted up her dress and flopped on the ground. He pulled down his pants and started to mount her. Just as the girl was a-guiding his tallywacker home, somebody tapped the city fellow on the shoulder.

"Excuse me, mister," says one of them big peckerwoods, "would you mind trading twitchets? It's pretty dark back there. I've made a mistake and picked my own sister!"

[X739.3.1]

Although the southern mountaineer is stereotyped as one who frequently violates the incest taboo (see Numbers 10, 39, and 53 of this collection), a tale such as this makes it clear that he is as conscientious in observing the taboo as anyone else, but at the same time he apparently is willing to joke about violating it more openly than most other people. Ernest Baughman informed Randolph that he had heard the story in Albuquerque in 1947, about Mexican migrant workers riding in a truck. Randolph himself makes note of a version, with a London setting, in Cerf, *Anything for a Laugh*, p. 205. Legman, *Rationale*, I, 461–

462, relates it as heard in San Francisco in 1943, with a sailor requesting a swap because he'd picked up an aunt of his.

34. Snake on the Bridge

Told by Ed Worden, Eureka Springs, Ark., November, 1948.
He heard it near Huntsville, Ark., about 1898.

One time there was two fellows going home from the tavern, and they was both pretty drunk. The fellow that led the way was six foot tall, and the little one carried a walking stick because his leg had got crippled. Just about midnight they come to the bridge, and the big fellow thought of an old saying about how it is healthy to piss in running water, so he started to take a leak.

The moon was a-shining, but it was pretty dark on the bridge, and the crippled fellow was about half blind anyhow. Soon as he seen the big man's tool a-flopping over the rail he hollered "Snake!" and whacked it with that there cane. The big man screeched like a wildcat, and grabbed his pecker with both hands. "Bust him again, Tom!" the big fellow yelled, "he's bit me!" They do say the big man never did know what really happened, because the crippled fellow was scared to speak up. There ain't no telling what that big drunk might do, if he found out somebody has hit his tally-whacker with a stick.

The boys around town thought it was a great joke, and for a long time after that they would holler "Snake!" at each other right on Main Street. Some other fellow would holler back, "Bust him again! He's bit me!" and then both of them would laugh. The womenfolks all heard the story, of course, but they had to act innocent like they didn't know what them boys meant. Probably that's why everybody thought it was so funny.

[J1838.1; X712.7.1]
Ernest Baughman stated that he heard this in Albuquerque in 1950. Randolph makes reference to two polite versions of the story, in which a toe is mistaken for a snake: Chase, *American Folk Tales and Songs*, pp. 92–93; and Lon Hogan, Springfield, Mo., *Daily News*, April 20, 1959. Still another "toe" version appears in White, ed., *The Frank C. Brown Collection of North Carolina Folklore*, I, 699. Legman, *Rationale*, II, 610, reports two "penis" versions from oral tradition: from Berkeley in 1942, and from London in 1954.

35. He Lost His Memory

Told by an elderly gentleman in Forsyth, Mo., August, 1940. He doesn't want his name mentioned in connection with this story.

One time there was a man named Jeff that was eighty-two years old, but mighty spry for his age. The young fellows was all surprised when they found out that Jeff still went a-hunting twice a week, and he could ride horses just as good as anybody. They was always joking about how Jeff run after the womenfolks, but nobody really believed it.

Some of the boys got to talking one day, and they all says it must be fine to be healthy like that, when a fellow is eighty-two years old. But Jeff just shook his head. "It ain't no fun to be old," he says, "because your memory always goes back on you." The boys just kind of kidded him along, and they says so long as a man can do a little fucking, it don't make no difference if he can remember things or not.

But old Jeff shook his head some more, and he says it makes a man look awful foolish. "Why, just last night I woke up with a hard-on," says he, "so I roused my wife to have a little fun. But Mary says for me to shut up, because we have already done it twice, not thirty minutes before. And there was two towels laying on the floor, so I knowed she was telling the truth." Jeff looked mighty gloomy. "It's kind of sad, when a man gets so old he can't remember things like that," says he.

Them young fellows just stared at Jeff goggle-eyed, but nobody said another word. The old man looked so solemn, they didn't rightly know if he was kidding 'em or not. It stands to reason that he was, but you can't never tell for sure.

[X735.7.1]

Legman, *Rationale*, I, 628, and *Rationale*, II, 648, cites this as a highly popular joke, widely and frequently collected since 1935; however, he offers only one example, from New York in 1952. At first glance, the tale would appear to belong more to that substantial group of absent-minded fool stories classified by Thompson, *Motif-Index*, under J2000–J2050, than to the category of sexual humor. But on the contrary, the old man is no fool; he simply *feels* foolish because of the embarrassment occasioned by his failing memory. In effect, the memory loss also serves as an indirect brag of sexual prowess.

36. That Boy Needs Pants

Told by Elbert Short, Crane, Mo., June, 1933. He heard it near Marionville, Mo., in the early 1900's.

One time there was some country folks giving a big dinner, with a lot of high-toned company from town. The house was kind of crowded, because they had too goddam many children. The kids was running all over the place, and hollering so loud the grown folks couldn't hardly hear theirself think.

There was one boy that climbed right up on the dinner table, so his mother had to pull him down by the collar. She didn't want to give him hell in front of the company, but the old man reached over and slapped his bottom good.

"Maw," says the farmer, "how old is that there boy?" The woman says he must be twelve, going on thirteen. "Well, I reckon we'll have to put pants on him," says the old man. "That's the second time he's crawled up there and drug his tallywhacker through the butter."

The high-toned company just set there, without saying a word. But everybody took notice they didn't eat no more butter.

[X712.6.1]

Randolph quotes from an article by May Kennedy McCord, Springfield, Mo., *News*, January 12, 1939: "Boys wore tail-shirts to school and everywhere, without pants, until about ten or twelve years old." In *Who Blowed Up the Church House*, pp. 93–94, Randolph relates an innocuous "shirttail boy" story, but remarks in his notes to the tale (pp. 207–208) that although there are many stories about "shirttail boys" in the Ozarks, the best of them are "unprintable."

37. Stuck in a Mud Hole

Told by Fred High, Berryville, Ark., October, 1953. A very old story, he says, heard in Carroll County, Ark., about 1895.

One time there was a man and his wife lived all by themselves. There was a freighter come along on the way to Little Rock, and he wanted to stay overnight because it was a-raining. All three of 'em had to sleep in one bed, but that wasn't nothing uncommon in them days.

Along in the night the woman got the freighter to crawl over and mount her, as she says her husband is sound asleep. Right in the middle of things, the freighter seen that the old man was a-waking up. So he begun to cluck and holler "Hup, Fanny! Whoa!" to make out like he was a-dreaming and didn't know where he was at.

The old man just opened one eye, but he seen what was going on, all right. The freighter was a-bouncing around on top of the woman, a-clucking and hollering like he was driving a team. Pretty soon the old man spoke up. "Stranger," says he, "it looks like you'll have to unload, before you can get out of that there mud hole."

Now ain't that a hell of a way for a man to talk, with the old woman a-fucking a freighter right before his eyes?

[X725.1.1]

In the words of Randolph's informant, "A very old story," indeed. It may be found in the fifteenth-century *One Hundred Merrie and Delightsome Stories* (ed. de la Sale), No. 7. A related story from France has appeared in *Kryptadia*, II, pp. 165–167, in which a traveler whose carriage is stuck in the mud stays with a farmer and his wife. He mounts the wife, and while copulating calls as if to his horses. The farmer thinks he is dreaming of pushing his carriage out of the mud. Legman, *Rationale*, I, 733, notes another related story, from the 1912 manuscript of W. L. McAtee, in which the husband tells his wife to warm the cold houseguest in bed. He then attributes the bed's continued shaking to his wife's not warming the guest quickly enough.

38. The Better End

*Told by J. L. Russell, Harrison, Ark., April, 1950. He heard
it near Green Forest, Ark., about 1890.*

One time there was a young widow-woman lived by herself,
and one of the town boys slipped out to see her. But while
he was there, her steady fellow come a-riding up the lane
on a sorrel horse. There wasn't no way for the town boy to
get out of the house right quick, so he climbed up into the
loft and hid.

Soon as the steady fellow come in, he grabbed the widow-
woman. Him and her just wrastled and squealed and rolled
and tumbled, like a couple of wild minks in rutting season.
He got the widow-woman's dress clear up over her head, and
she didn't have nothing on underneath. That widow-woman
knowed tricks that these country girls never heard tell of.
And all this time the town boy was peeking through a knot-
hole where he could see everything.

The town boy's head was a-spinning like a top, and he
didn't know if he was afoot or horseback. The widow-woman
giggled just then, and she says, "Don't squeeze me so hard."
But her steady fellow let out a whoop. "I got a notion to
squeeze you plumb in two," he says. The town boy couldn't
keep still no longer. "Throw me the end with the pussy in
it!" says he.

The story don't say what happened after that. But it stands
to reason there was the devil to pay and no pitch hot, as any
fool can plainly see.

[J2368]
Ernest Baughman reported to Randolph that he heard a similar story of newlyweds in Indiana in 1935. The woman undresses
behind a screen, putting her wig, glass eye, and wooden leg on a
table where her new husband can see them. He calls to her to

throw him the part he wants. Baughman's form of the tale is noted in Aarne-Thompson, *Type Index,* under Type 1379*, "False Members," with the husband asking for a buttock to use as a pillow. The story also appears in Hall, *Anecdota,* I, No. 261, as well as in two variants in Lockridge, *Waggish Tales,* pp. 80–85.

In another variant, which I heard as a Navy man in the Pacific in 1945, two men claim to have been accepted by the same girl, and the dispute finally goes to court. The judge, emulating the wisdom of Solomon, sees dividing the girl as the only solution, and asks each man what he prefers. One eulogizes her beautiful eyes, hair, lips, etc.; the other says, "Just give me the part with the hole in it."

39. A Good Dose of Clap

Told by Dwight Swain, Norman, Okla., November, 1953. He heard it in northwest Arkansas. Otho Pratt, of Fort Madison, Iowa, collected a similar tale near Galena, Mo., in the 1920's.

One time there was a country boy come a-walking into town, and he made a bee-line for the whore house. The woman begun to tell what pretty girls she had upstairs, but the boy didn't pay her no mind. "I don't care nothing about that," says he, "all I want is a good dose of clap." The woman figured the fellow must have went crazy. "What on earth do you want to get the clap for?" she asked him. "So I can give it to Sis," says the boy. The woman that run the whore house was pretty tough, but she wasn't used to such talk as that. "My God," she says, "what did your sister do to you?"

The country boy looked surprised. "Sis? Why she never did nothing. Me and her gets along fine. But she'll give it to Paw, before the week's out." The woman just stood there with her mouth open, and she thought the whole thing is terrible. "Good Lord," she says, "your Paw must be awful mean to you!" The country boy stared at her. "No," says he, "Paw's all right. I just want him to give Maw a good dose." The woman that run the place was plumb shocked when she heard that. "It's a awful thing for a boy to hate his own mother," she says.

"Why, I ain't got nothing against Maw," says the boy. "You ain't?" hollered the woman that run the whore house. "Then what for do you want her to get the clap?" The country boy scowled. "Why," says he, "she'll give it to that goddam preacher, that put me out of the Sunday School. He's the son-of-a-bitch I'm after!"

[Z49.1.1]
Ernest Baughman informed Randolph that he had heard this in Indiana in 1930. It also appears in Hall, *Anecdota*, I, No. 182. In *Anecdota*, II, No. 494, it is related again, but instead of a minister, Prince Henry of Navarre and Louis XIV are named as victims of the trick.

Legman, *Rationale*, I, 740, notes that in Voltaire's *Candide* Pangloss recounts a similar chain of transmission when Candide finds him as a horrible, disease-ridden beggar. However, this lacks the revenge motif, the earliest form of which Legman traces to McAtee's 1912 manuscript in an item called "Bill's Revenge," which claims to be based on a popular tale (*Rationale*, II, 318). He also notes another minister-as-victim version, related by a Cleveland physician on a transcontinental train in 1938.

40. He Had Three Sizes

Told by Bob Wyrick, Eureka Springs, Ark., March, 1950. He heard it near Green Forest, Ark., about 1900.

One time a young fellow was going to marry a girl up on Panther Creek, but they hadn't done no screwing yet. The girl seen him taking a leak out behind the barn, so then she begun to holler that the wedding will have to be called off. "You're a-carrying more than I can take," she says, "that thing is too big for a little girl like me!" But the young fellow just laughed. "I've got three of 'em," says he. "One is lady size, another'n is whore size, and the third is mare size. I always use the mare size to piss with."

So the girl says all right, and they got married right away. The first night she tried the lady size, and everything went fine. The second night she latched onto the whore size, and that was wonderful, too. The third night she called for the mare size, and it was the best of all. Him and her both had a good time, and you'd think they would live happy ever after.

About three weeks after the wedding, the girl woke up one morning, and she just laid there and yawned. "Honey," she says, "fetch me one of them garters that is hanging on the chair." The young fellow just grinned at her. "You ain't got no stockings on," says he. "What do you want with a garter?" The girl yawned again, and snuggled up against him. "I just thought of something," she says. "If we can tie all three of them pricks together, maybe I could get a *good* fucking for a change!"

[X735.1.1.1]

A variant of this tale collected in Belgium is published in *Kryptadia,* IV, 323–324. Another variant appears in Afanasiev, *Stories,* pp. 35–38, in which a bride-to-be thinks of how much more pleasurable intercourse could be if a man had multiple penises which could be twisted together. Two other variant forms also come from Belgium: *Kryptadia,* IV, 319–321, 324–325. In one, a man who has lost his penis receives the gift of a stallion from his father-in-law. He notices the stallion's member and wishes he had one like it. Miraculously, he is so provided, and he tells his wife. She berates her father for not having given him the biggest stallion. In the second, the bridegroom tells his new wife that his testicles are called "the show." After their first bout in bed, she tells him to put in "the show" as well. Legman, *Rationale*, I, 141–144, makes reference to a number of tales and jokes in which the man possesses multiple penises.

41. Tacking On Her Maidenhead

Told by J. L. Russell, Harrison, Ark., April, 1950. He heard it about 1900.

One time there was a fellow fooling with a young country girl. She told him that her folks did not believe in screwing, but he finally got his pecker into her anyhow. "This ain't screwing at all," says he, "because I am just tacking on your maidenhead." And so she says maybe it is all right.

The girl was kind of uneasy at first, but pretty soon she says, "This here tacking is wonderful, and I believe it's a-doing me good!" They sure had a fine time, until four o'clock in the morning. Finally he wanted to go home, but the girl kept a-hollering, "Tack it again, Henry! Tack it again!" The fellow told her they better wait till tomorrow night. "I can't do no more tacking now," says he, "because I have run out of thread."

At that the girl began to cry, because she thought the fellow didn't love her no more. "You ain't out of thread, Henry," she says. "Why, just a minute ago I felt two great big balls of yarn, a-bouncing up against my ass!"

[K1363.6; X735.9.5]
Randolph notes that the word "tack" refers to the short stitches which fasten the top of a heavy quilt or comforter to the lining, and the "tacking" is usually done with colored yarns. Variants of this tale are listed in Aarne-Thompson, *Type Index*, under Type 1542**, "The Maiden's Honor," in which the

mother tells the girl to guard her honor, and the tailor later promises to sew up her "honor." Further versions also have been collected both in France (*Kryptadia,* II, 5–7) and in Belgium (*Kryptadia,* IV, 326–329). Legman, *Rationale,* I, 333–334, points out that the element of the boy pleading that he is out of thread and the girl observing that he has two balls of yarn hanging there goes back to Béroalde de Verville, *Le Moyen de Parvenir* (1610), ch. 31. He also notes that the story is given in the erotic novel, *The Way of a Virgin,* 1928 [?].

42. The Double-Action Sailor

Told by Frank S. Bates, Argenta, Ark., August, 1940.

One time there was a sailor come to this town, and he had ribbons on his uniform. And also his pants was buttoned at both sides, instead of in front. Pretty soon he propositioned one of the town girls, but she says no. "I don't never fool with strangers," says she. "What could you give me, that the home boys ain't got?"

The Navy fellow looked kind of surprised. "Lady," says he, "it must be you don't know about sea-faring men. These farmer boys ain't got only one pecker apiece, but I've got two." The girl never heard of such a thing before. "You've got two tallywhackers?" she says. The fellow told her yes, and he says all sailors is built double-action that way, on account of the government regulations. "This I've got to see," says the girl, and down the road they went.

Soon as she come to the brickyard the girl rolled over and pulled up her clothes. The sailor unbuttoned his pants on the right side, and he sure did give her a good screwing. Then they both laid there and rested awhile. Pretty soon she says, "Well, let's try the other one." So he unbuttoned his pants on the left side, and pulled it out. But the goddam thing just hung down, limp as a rag. "Look at that now," says the sailor, "a-sulking because he didn't get to go first!" The girl just set there a minute, and then she laughed till the tears run down her face.

She busted out laughing the next night too, when the navy fellow wanted to take her out again. But she wouldn't go with him. "Sailors is educational, and I wouldn't have missed it for anything," she says. "But when it comes to steady company, these single-action country boys is good enough for me."

[X712.2.3.1]
The humor of this story hinges on the style of sailors' trousers, which, until after World War II, were fastened by a row of buttons on each side. Legman, *Rationale*, I, 143, gives a related story, heard in New York in 1950. A hobo's penis keeps falling out of various holes in his unpatched pants. The housewife who is giving him a handout marvels at the number of pricks he has. The theme is deceptive suggestion of multiple organs, and of course is related to the many other tales of multiple penises (see Number 40 of this collection, "He Had Three Sizes").

43. A Peck of Trouble

Told by Clyde Sharp, Pack, Mo., August, 1928.

One time Randy Braxton was a-walking down the road, and he met up with Bay Smithers, that used to be Justice of the Peace. "Howdy, Squire," says Randy. "How's everything up your way?"

Bay just shook his head, because he was feeling mighty low. "Not very good, Randy," says he. "My daughter has took down with typhoid fever, and the old woman's a-dying of consumption. I sure got a peck o' trouble."

Randy looked mighty solemn. "It sure is too bad, Squire," he says. "I don't know nothing about typoid fever, and there ain't no consumption in our family, neither. But when it comes to pecker trouble, I sure can sympathize with you!"

[J1805.1.2]

There are many stories based on an unintentional pun, that is, the misunderstanding of a simple word or phrase. In Lockridge, *Waggish Tales,* pp. 200–201, a woman wearing a tight skirt is late to church. As she approaches the church, she asks a boy, "Is Mass out yet?" He answers, "It soon will be if you take any longer steps." In *Kryptadia,* IV, 380–381 (from France), the priest tells the girl in the confessional, "Ne péchez plus" (sin no more); she thinks he says, "Ne pissez plus" (piss no more). See also Number 47 of this collection, "The Kids Didn't Catch It."

44. No Use to Rattle the Blind

Told by Ross Coleman, Eureka Springs, Ark., November, 1953. He heard it near Green Forest, Ark., about 1910.

One time there was a woman that had a good home and a baby and a new piano, but another fellow used to lay up with her while her husband was away. She told him to rattle the window-blind, and if the coast was clear she would get up and let him in. Well, one night the woman and her man was a-setting by the fire, and the window-blind begun to rattle. She was afraid he might suspicion something, because there wasn't no wind blowing. So the woman jumped up and begun to play the piano, and then she sung out:

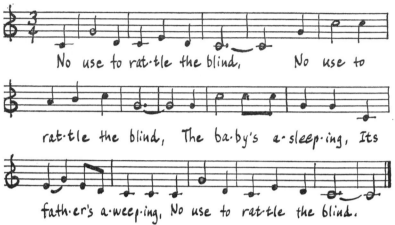

No use to rat·tle the blind, No use to rat·tle the blind, The ba·by's a·sleep·ing, Its fath·er's a·weep·ing, No use to rat·tle the blind.

The woman's husband wasn't such a fool as them people thought, and he seen how things was, all right. "Get your ass out of my way," says he, and pushed her off the piano-stool. Then he begun to pound on the keys like a cyclone a-coming, and he sung out:

> No use to rattle the blind,
> No use to rattle the blind,
> The baby's a-sucking,
> And I'll do my own fucking,
> No use to rattle the blind.

Him and her just set there and looked at each other after that, but there wasn't nary a word spoke. The window-blind didn't rattle no more, neither. Some folks say the fellow that done it was so scared he run clear out of the country, and never did come back to the house where they had the new piano.

K1546

Aarne-Thompson, *Type Index*, lists this as Type 1419H, "Woman Warns Lover of Husband by Singing Song," and notes, among other examples, Boccaccio's *Decameron,* Day VII, Tale 1. French versions have also been collected; *Kryptadia,* II, 115–117, and *Kryptadia,* X, 110–112. In his *Type and Motif-Index of the Folktales of England and North America* (K1546.1), Baughman gives several more American versions: from New Jersey, Halpert, *JAF,* LV, 137–40; from North Carolina, Boggs, *JAF,* XLVII, 304, 305; and from South Carolina (a Negro version), Smiley, *JAF,* XXXII, 363. Randolph himself published another version, collected in Branson, Mo., in 1938, in *The Devil's Pretty Daughter,* pp. 14–15, in which he believes that his informant "cleaned up" the husband's song. Legman, *Rationale,* I, 799–801, notes further references: Walter Anderson, *Der Schwank vom Alten Hildebrand* (1931), p. 324; C. R. Baskerville, *PMLA,* XXXVI, 590–592; *Histoires Arabes* (1927), 208–209. He also expresses the belief that it is "the *cante fable* most strongly surviving and still most commonly collected in the Anglo-American tradition."

45. Lady's Choice

Told by Miss Beulah S. Sherwood, Warsaw, Mo., January, 1946.

One time old man Struther's boy married the prettiest girl in the whole country. He was a good hard-working farmer, and it looked like they would maybe do all right. But in about six months the pretty girl walked out on him. Then she got a divorce, and married young Jack Sergeant. Jack was a big handsome fellow, but kind of ornery and shiftless. Mostly he just hung around the pool-hall in town.

Old man Struther was all broke up when his boy's wife got the divorce. And when she married Jack Sergeant, the old man was fit to be tied. He says a woman must be crazy to leave a hard-working husband with a good bottom farm, and take up with a loafer that ain't got a pot to piss in nor a window to throw it out.

It was right in front of the post office that old man Struther run into the pretty girl, and she says "Hello" just like they was good friends. The old man started to walk on past her, but all of a sudden he stopped. "Lucy," says he, "will you answer me one question?" The pretty girl just smiled at him, and nodded her head. "Well," he says, "you've done left my boy, and married Jack Sergeant. What I want to know is, how much better off are you?" The pretty girl kind of giggled. "How much? Oh, about four-and-a-half inches," she says. And then the pretty girl walked on down the street, a-wiggling her ass the way they do nowadays.

Old man Struther just stood there for a minute. Then he got in his buggy and went back home. But from that day on, nobody ever heard him say another word about the pretty girl that got the divorce.

[X712.2.1.1]
This story develops out of the belief, still held by many (if not most) men, that a girl desires a large penis to be sexually satisfied. The theme recurs in many variants: see Numbers 25, 40, 49, 66, 75, and 86 of this collection. The widely known erotic song, "The Bastard King of England," in which an intended castration results instead in a lengthened penis, also makes use of the theme.

46. He Done the Right Thing

Told by Joe Ingenthron, Forsyth, Mo., June, 1940. A very old story, he said.

One time there was a country boy come to the ice-house place at Forsyth, where they don't allow no square dancing, and everybody was doing round dances. He didn't know any of the girls, but there was a good-looking woman setting on a bench, so he asked her to dance with him. But she says no. The country boy was not used to women acting like that, so he says, "Well, you can kiss my ass!"

The woman told her husband what the country boy said, and he come out on the porch. "You go back in there and apologize to my wife," says he, "otherwise I will beat the living shit out of you!" The country boy seen he didn't have no chance, because the woman's husband was a great big man. So he went back in the room where they was having the dance. "Ma'am," says he, "you don't need to kiss my ass, after all. Me and your husband has made other arrangements."

[J1365]
Randolph notes a similar tale collected by Richard M. Dorson, in Michigan, *JAF*, LXI, 126–127. Another version appears in Hall, *Anecdota*, I, No. 452.

47. The Kids Didn't Catch It

Told by Richard Pilant, Eureka Springs, Ark., January, 1949. He heard it at Granby, Mo., about 1920.

One time there was a fellow walking home from town, and he seen some Holy Rollers having a meeting in a grove. He was a man that didn't have much use for religion, but these people was singing and picking guitars, so he stopped to listen at them. It wasn't no time till he was patting his foot, and then he begun to stomp with both feet, and pretty soon the Power got a-hold of him. So then he started to dance and roll and holler just like the rest of 'em. They seen he was coming through, and the elders all begun to pray for his salvation.

The fellow's wife got kind of worried when he didn't come home, so she sent her two little boys to see what become of him. Pretty soon they come a-running back, hollering that their pappy is just about dead. So the kids told her they seen him laying on the ground, with a big crowd of people standing there, and everybody says "the old shit's a-dyin'." The woman slapped the boys good for talking like that about their pappy, and she says they ought to be ashamed. Then she got her shawl and went down the road to see what was a-going on.

When she got to the meeting the fellow was setting on a stump, and the preachers all shaking hands with him. "Have you been sick?" says she. The fellow says, "Of course not. There ain't nothing the matter, only I got a little touch of religion." So then she told him what the kids said. "I laid on the ground awhile," says he, "but there wasn't nothing said about me a-dying. And nobody called me an old shit, neither." And then the fellow says he will whip them boys within a inch of their life, soon as he gets home.

Just about that time a woman was took with the Power, and fell down. The preachers and elders run over there to pray for her, and pretty soon everybody begun to sing "The Old Ship of Zion." The fellow looked at his wife, and grinned kind of sheepish. "I reckon that's what the boys heard," says he. "Our children ain't much used to gospel songs, and that's why they didn't quite ketch the meaning." The woman listened to the singing awhile. "It sounds pretty much like what the boys said, don't it?" she giggled. So then him and her just walked on home, and the kids didn't get no licking, neither.

[J1805.1.3]
As in Number 43, "A Peck of Trouble," the humor in this story hinges on a misunderstanding of a word or phrase. Ernest Baughman informed Randolph of a group of similar tales based

on misunderstanding of hymns: Constipated Cross-eyed Bear (A Consecrated Cross I'd Bear), My Feet Stink on the Mantel (I'm Feasting on the Manna), Jesus Is Sneaking through Humboldt Park (Jesus Is Seeking a Humble Heart). It is not made clear whether these are actual or would-be tales. The distorting of tales of all kinds into gross puns has long been an exercise in linguistic cleverness among children and not a few adults.

48. Wind on His Guts

Told by Elizabeth Maddocks, Joplin, Mo., June, 1937. She heard the tale in Christian County, Mo., about 1900.

One time there was a farmer that always had wind on his guts, till he was pooched out like a cat full of kittens. He could belch the loudest you ever heard, and whenever he let a fart it would stink something terrible. Finally he fired off a big one about four o'clock in the morning, so his wife jumped up and run out of the house. The kids run out too, and they all stood around in the yard a-puking till sun-up.

It took most of the morning to get the house aired out so they could make some coffee, and after she drunk it the old woman spoke up. "I can't stand no more of this," she says. "If you don't go see the doctor, me and the kids are going to leave here, and live with my folks." There was considerable grumbling and high words, but after while the fellow rode into town.

When he got to the doctor's office the farmer says, "Doc, there must be something wrong with my innards. Whenever I happen to break wind, it stinks so bad that nobody can't stay in the house with me." Doc Holton thought awhile, and then he says, "Do you reckon you could poot a little right now?" The fellow just drawed a deep breath, and then he turned loose a blast that pretty near unjointed him. Doc didn't say nothing, but he jumped up to open the windows, and the transom over the back door. Then he throwed the front door wide open, and the people that was waiting in the office all went out to get some fresh air.

"My God," says Doc, "something must have crawled up in you and died!" The fellow says he wants a bottle of strong medicine, but Doc just shook his head. "Medicine won't do no good," he says. "But I advise you to take a big dish of raw onions with every meal, and a lot of garlic, and maybe some wild ramps. And at night, just before you go to bed, you better eat half a pound of limberger cheese."

The poor farmer turned kind of green around the gills. "Do you reckon that stuff will cure me?" he says. Doc Holton looked mighty solemn. "No, I don't believe it will cure you," says he, "but it might help *some!*"

[X716.6.1]

Ernest Baughman told Randolph of a similar story heard in Indiana in 1937, about a doctor who told a woman with halitosis to eat shit. This is almost identical to that printed in a rare joke book, *The Stag Party,* of about 1890.

In addition to the gross cure, or non-cure, there is a second element to this tale, that of the unbearable smell of the person's breaking wind. See Numbers 51 and 65 of this collection for further examples, as well as Lockridge, *Waggish Tales,* pp. 151–152; Hall, *Anecdota,* II, No. 401; and Legman, *Rationale,* II, 890.

49. It Was a Tee-Hee

Told by Lon Jordan, Farmington, Ark., December, 1941. He said the hero of the tale lived at Fayetteville, Ark., about 1910.

One time there was a man that wanted a good wife, and he figured out a way to tell if anybody is a virgin or not. Whenever he seen a girl that looked all right, he took her out buggy riding. All of a sudden he would unbutton his pants and show her his tool. "What's that?" says he. "Why, it's a pecker," the girl says. So then he would button up his pants. "You ain't what I'm looking for," says he, and back to town they went.

He kept on like that for several years, but all the girls give him the same answer. Finally he found a pretty little waitress with yellow hair, that worked in the hotel. They went buggy riding, and when he pulled out his tallywhacker she just kind of giggled. "Why, that's a tee-hee!" she says. Right then and there the fellow knowed she was just what he wanted. So him and her got married, and they was both mighty happy.

About six months after the wedding, they got to talking about old times. "Honey," says he, "how did you come to call my tool a tee-hee, that first time we went out buggy riding?" Why, she says, tee-hee is the right name for it, and any other girl would tell you the same. "No," says he, "out where I was raised they call it a pecker." The girl just laughed. "Shucks," she says, "them cornfed floozies ain't been around much. Why, everybody knows a pecker is bigger than that!"

[X712.4.2]

Randolph notes that he has a slightly different version that circulated in Yell County, Ark., in the 1930's. Ernest Baughman reported to Randolph a version from Albuquerque in 1955. A similar story was also collected in France; *Kryptadia*, X, 27–32. Legman, *Rationale*, I, 331, 535–536, offers several close versions, as well as variant forms. One, employing the term "wee-wee" instead of "tee-hee," was heard in California in 1939. From both Idaho and New York, in 1952, the bridegroom identifies his organ to his bride as a "penis," and she responds by observing that a "penis" must be like a prick, only smaller. Variants often take the form of direct insults to the man. In one from Idaho in 1919, the groom tells the bride not to peek as he undresses (a reversal of the usual roles). The bride, referring to her short,

starched nightgown, says, "Oh, it's a little short stiff one!" The
groom accuses, "You went and peeked after all!"

50. The Call to Preach

*Told by Leo McKellops, Anderson, Mo., May, 1933. An old
story, known in many parts of Missouri and Arkansas.*

One time there was a fellow come walking into town, a-hollering how he's going to quit farming and preach the gospel. He
was just a big country boy, all pecker and feet, the kind of a
fellow that couldn't find his butt with both hands in broad
daylight. Anybody could see he didn't know enough to pour
piss out of a boot, with directions printed on the heel. But
he stood right up in meeting anyhow, and told everybody
he had a call to preach.

"I was a-plowing the south forty," says he, "and all of a
sudden there come a bolt of lightning, and the loudest thunder you ever heard. It knocked me down onto my knees, and
I prayed for a sign. Pretty soon I seen a big smoke in the
heavens, in the shape of the letter *P*. I just kept on a-praying,
and then I seen the letter *C*. Them letters *PC* can't mean
nothing only *Preach Christ,* so that's what I am to do!"

Some of the folks kind of grinned when they heard that,
but everybody waited to see what the regular preacher thought
about it. The preacher says right off that he don't doubt the
young man's word, but a call to preach is a serious matter,
and it is best not to do nothing hasty. "I'll have to take it to
the Lord in prayer," says he. So they all prayed awhile, and
then the preacher says "Brother, the feeling of this congregation is that you ain't called to preach, because you have mis-
took the meaning of the sign. The letters *PC* mean *Plow
Corn,* and I believe that's what you better do," says the

preacher. So then every one of them old deacons says "Amen!" and that's all there was to it.

The big country boy grumbled some because he couldn't get no license to preach, but the fellows down at the tavern give him a few glasses of beer, and pretty soon he got to feeling better. "That stuff about letters in the sky is just a made-up tale," says he. "I got a call to preach, all right. But it wouldn't do to tell them folks down at the church house."

So then the fellows at the tavern give him a lot more beer, and finally one of 'em says, "What makes you think you're called to be a preacher?" The country boy just grinned kind of foolish. "Well, I got the biggest prick in the neighborhood," says he, "and a terrible craving for fried chicken."

The crowd all laughed when they heard that, but after the country boy had went home they got to talking about it more serious. Book learning ain't everything, and neither is slick manners and fine clothes. If they'd give that big country boy a chance, may he would have made a good preacher, sure enough.

[X459.1.1; X712.2.1.2]

Randolph notes that Brewer, *The Word on the Brazos,* pp. 69–70, gives a Negro version from Texas. The story is a natural development out of the stereotype of the uneducated backwoods preacher, who is consistently characterized as fortuitously visiting when one of his parishioners is having chicken for dinner (as in the long popular Snuffy Smith comic strip), and as having a penchant for seducing female members of the congregation (see Number 17 of this collection, "The Two Preachers").

51. They Got Acquainted

Told by Bob Wyrick, Eureka Springs, Ark., March, 1950.

One time there was a country boy got on the train, and he was going to Harrison. There wasn't nobody else in the car only a town girl, but she acted kind of stuck up, so the boy did not say nothing to her. Pretty soon they come past a place where some people had a slaughter-house down by the creek. There was always a terrible stink around a slaughter-house in them days, and the wind blowed it right into the cars.

The town girl wrinkled up her nose, and then she pulled out one of them little handkerchiefs with lace on it. "My goodness!" she says. "What is that awful smell?"

The country boy figured this was a good chance to say something comical, so they could get acquainted. "I reckon the conductor must have let a fart," says he. The town girl looked mighty scornful. "I didn't get on this train to be insulted!" she says.

"Neither did I," says the country boy. "If he farts again, let's you and me get off, and walk home through the brush!" The girl couldn't help laughing when she heard that, and the ice was broke right there. So then they got to talking, and pretty soon the boy stuck his hand up under her dress. Him and her was right friendly, by the time they got to Harrison.

[X716.6.2]
Randolph's informant also told him a related story in which it was the girl who broke wind. To hide her embarrassment, she asked another passenger on the train for a newspaper. His answer was that he had no newspaper but would get her a handful of cobs as soon as the train stopped. A version closer to that given here appears in Hall, *Anecdota*, I, No. 380, with the setting in a restaurant rather than on a train. Legman, *Rationale*, II, 866–

867, notes variant forms from Washington, D.C., in 1944, and from a nineteenth-century British jest book, in which the woman comes out with the snappy reply.

52. A Good Coon Dog

Told by Frank Hembree, Galena, Mo., April, 1945.

One time there was a fellow from Springfield that wanted a tree-dog to hunt coons, and he met up with Jim Stottsworth down at the livery barn. Soon as the howdies was over, Jim offered to sell him old Bugler, for sixty-five dollars. Everybody knows that a good coon hound has always got a big asshole, and so the fellow from Springfield started a-feeling under old Bugler's tail. "This dog seems kind of tight," says he.

Them Stottsworth boys knowed all the answers, particular when it come to varmint hounds and things like that. "We went squirrel-hunting yesterday," says Jim, "so naturally I tightened old Bugler up a little. But he'll be back to regular coon-size in a day or two."

The fellow from Springfield just looked at Jim Stottsworth for a minute, and then he got in his buggy and drove off down the road. The boys at the livery barn figured maybe the fellow would come back and buy old Bugler after all, but he never did.

[H1589]
This appears to be a local anecdote limited to the southern United States, where raccoon hunting is popular, both as a sport and to help fill the family larder. Randolph himself notes two other versions; one, collected by Herbert Halpert from John Jacob Niles of Kentucky (*Hoosier Folklore Bulletin*, I, 63), has

the dog's nose screwed down for squirrels; the other, from Franklin Allen, Joplin, Mo., November, 1957, has the dog's ass screwed down for squirrels. Both versions state that a wrench goes along with the dog. In *Rationale*, II, 821–822, Legman relates the same story about a bear dog, as told by a traveling salesmen on a train in Texas in 1945.

53. He Called the Wedding Off

Told by Mrs. Mary Alice Blake, Monett, Mo., July, 1946. It was a common story around Monett, she says in the late 1930's.

One time there was a fellow from Oklahoma a-telling jokes down at the store, and finally he says, "What is a Arkansas virgin?" There was considerable talk about it, and then the fellow says, "Well, it's a girl that can out-run all her brothers." The home boys all laughed like hell when they heard that, but there was a big farmer from Arkansas come in the store just then, and he got mad.

Soon as they throwed the big farmer out in the street, another fellow got to telling about the Arkansas boy that was fixing to get married. But just a few days before the wedding, he says the whole thing is called off. The boy's old man wanted to know what has went wrong all of a sudden. "Paw," says the boy, "I been feeling around in Fanny's pants, and I found out she's a virgin. That's why I decided not to marry her."

The old man was considerable set back, because he never figured on anything like that. "You done right, son," says he. "If that girl ain't good enough for her own kinfolks, she ain't good enough for us, neither!"

The folks used to tell lots of them funny stories, specially in Missouri towns that lays pretty close to the Arkansas line.

But it seems like pretty near everybody in Arkansas is kind of ill tempered, and they can't take a joke. Some say it's because them people don't eat nothing but sowbelly and huckleberries, that makes 'em fight when the sun gets hot. There ain't hardly a day passes, in the summer time, that some of them big Arkansawyers don't come over here a-looking for trouble.

[X722.1.1]
Ernest Baughman reported to Randolph having heard the story in Indiana in 1934. Randolph also notes a version in which the boy shoots the girl upon discovering that she is a virgin, followed by the same tag-line from the father, in Elgart, *Over Sexteen,* p. 100. Buehler, in his master's thesis, pp. 47–48, gives a version similar to Elgart's from an Illinois informant. He also refers to versions in the Indiana University Folklore Archives (from Birmingham, Mich., 1954) and in Curran, *Clean Dirt,* p. 188; in both the bride is shot upon discovery that she is a virgin. Legman, *Rationale,* I, 460–461, discourses on the mockery of the virgin bride concept and notes two versions (from New York, 1940, and La Jolla, Calif., 1965) in which the girl, as in Randolph's version, is simply spurned because she is not good enough for her own family. A related story appears in Hall, *Anecdota,* I, No. 376. The groom, upon discovering that he has married a virgin, refuses to have anything to do with her. She sneers that he wants someone else to do the dirty work, and then he'll take all the pleasure. He answers that he didn't build the subway, but he rides in it.

54. Pulling Out Hairs

Told by Frank Shelton, Fayetteville, Ark., May, 1952. He heard it in Yell County, Ark., about 1930.

One time there was a young fellow a-walking through the country, and he stopped at some people's house to stay all night. There wasn't nobody lived there but an old man and his wife, so they only had one bed. The old man slept in the middle, with his wife on one side and the traveler on the other.

It was about midnight when the woman says, "Come on over," but the traveler was afraid the old man might wake up. "My husband is a awful sound sleeper," says the woman, "just pull a hair out of his ass, if you don't believe it." The young fellow pulled out a hair just like she said, but the old man went right on a-snoring. So then the traveler went over and give the woman what she wanted.

After while the woman says "Come on over" again. The young fellow wasn't so anxious this time, but she finally got him in the notion. He pulled another hair out of the old man's ass, and the old man kept right on a-snoring. So then the traveler crawled over again, and give the woman what she wanted.

The third time the woman says "Come on over" the traveler didn't want to go, and he says, "We better let well enough alone." But the woman kept on fooling around till she got him in the notion again. So finally the young fellow jerked out another hair, and this time the old man woke up. "Stranger," says he, "I don't mind people fucking my wife. But you'll have to quit using my ass for a tally-board!"

[X725.1.2]

Hall, *Anecdota*, II, No. 277, gives the same story, except that the husband doesn't complain about being used as a tally-board until the sixteenth hair is pulled out. Abrahams, *Deep Down in the Jungle*, pp. 220–221, gives a version from black tradition in Philadelphia; the visitor is the familiar traveling salesman, and the woman is the host's daughter rather than his wife. Legman, *Rationale*, I, 773–774, notes that he heard it among children in Pennsylvania about 1930. He also points out a "cleaned up" version in a volume entitled, *And One Flew into the Cuckold's Nest*

(1966, p. 23), in which chest hairs are pulled out. A variant from Belgium (*Kryptadia,* IV, 303–305) describes the priest pulling hairs out of the sacristan's testicles before going to the servant's bed.

55. The Preacher and the Lady

Told by Pete Woolsey, Pineville, Mo., September, 1924.

One time there was a widow-woman named Hale that lived up on Coon Creek, and the other women didn't like her, but the menfolks all thought she was wonderful. There was men right here in town that would sneak out and leave their wife pretty near every night, and old Jim Butterfield used to lock up his store and go see the widow in broad daylight. Them fellows burnt up the Coon Creek road all the time, and they didn't care who knowed it, neither.

The womenfolks all says the widow Hale ought to be throwed in jail, but the sheriff wouldn't do nothing, because he was pussy-simple too. So then a bunch of church people went to see the preacher, which his name was Wilkes. They wanted him to tell the widow woman she better behave herself, or else move away. Because if she don't, the decent women is going to give the widow Hale a horse-whipping, and then run her out of the country. Old preacher Wilkes grumbled a good deal, but finally he says he'll go up on Coon Creek and see about it.

They didn't have no cars in them days, but young Park Chambers took the preacher out there in his new buggy. When they got to the widow Hale's cabin Park just waited outside, and old man Wilkes was gone a long time. Finally he come back out, a-shaking his head. "Mistress Hale is a good Christian woman," he says, "cultured and refined the best you ever seen! I don't understand why the ladies are telling all them bad stories about her!"

So then the preacher just stood there, a-looking back at the widow woman's house on Coon Creek. "All right, Reverend," says young Park Chambers. "Just button up your pants, and we'll get home in time for dinner."

[X433]

Randolph feels that this story must be old and widely known, and mentions once having heard it related in Yiddish by a Chicago girl in the wilds of Arkansas. He also cites a version in *Anecdota Americana* (1943), pp. 140–141, which was actually taken from the original Hall, *Anecdota*, I, No. 349. Legman, too, in *Rationale*, II, 219–20, considers it among the oldest of jokes, going back at least as far as the fifteenth-century Talmudic *Pirké Avoth*.

56. She Grabbed the Saddle-Horn

Told by Allen McQuary, Galena, Mo., December, 1935. He heard it "thirty or forty years ago" in Newton County, Ark.

One time there was a pretty girl lived out west of Neosho, and young Tom Harper was fetching her home from a dance. You know how they done it in them days. A boy just had one saddle-horse, and the girl used to climb on behind him. Sometimes he would make the horse cut up a little, and then she had to put her arms around the boy's waist to keep from getting throwed off.

Tom was a-riding a pretty lively pony that night, and maybe he used the spur a little bit. Him and the girl was both red-faced and panting when they got to her house. The next morning she kept telling the folks about what a wild ride they had through the woods. "I would have fell off sure," she says, "only I throwed my arms around Tom and held onto the saddle-horn."

The girl's old pappy listened at her a-talking, and after while he called her out where he was setting in the front yard. "Daughter," says he, "if I was you, I wouldn't say no more about holding onto the saddle-horn." The pretty girl says that's exactly what happened, and surely there ain't no harm in telling the truth. The old man just kind of winked at her. "Daughter," he says, "what you had a-hold of is your own business, and I ain't asking any questions. But everybody knows that Tom Harper rides a McClellan saddle."

The pretty girl turned red as a beet when she heard that, because the McClellan is an old-style army saddle, and there ain't no horn on it. After while she just grinned a little, and went back in the house. She never said another word about that wild ride through the woods with Tom Harper, neither.

[X712.7.2]
Ernest Baughman told Randolph of a version he had heard in Indiana in 1943, in which a boy carries a girl in a bathing suit on the bar of his bicycle. She notices later that he has a girl's bicycle. Everyone, of course, knows that a girl's bicycle has no cross bar. Randolph's story fails as a joke in this respect, for unless the listener is well versed about saddles, he needs the explanation that the McClellan saddle has no pommel, or horn. Buehler, in his master's thesis, pp. 54–56, collected it from an Indiana informant, with the woman riding behind an Indian, who yells "Yahoo" when she grabs the saddle horn to mount and dismount. Afterward, she finds that the Indian is riding bareback. Legman, *Rationale*, I, 288–290, gives a similar form of the story and states that it has been repeatedly collected in America since 1942. He also relates the bicycle version, with a London setting, as collected in New York in 1942. He feels that the original goes back to *Tom Brown's Jester* (1755; 1860 ed.), pp. 55–56, in which the

girl, responding to her father's question about what is the fastest-growing thing, asserts that it is the pommel of a saddle. She explains that when she rode behind the family servant, the pommel, when she first took hold, was no bigger than her finger, and that in less than a minute it was thicker than her wrist.

57. The Old Ral Hole

Told by Mrs. Ethel Barnes, Hot Springs, Ark., March, 1938.

One time there was a Yankee with long whiskers, also he had lost his manhood so the family sent him to Hot Springs. "It ain't nothing but the neuralgia," says he. But the doctor knowed what was the matter, all right. The Hot Springs policeman put him in the Old Ral bath-house, because it costs a lot of money to stay at the big hotel.

While him and some other fellows was taking the cure, they got to talking about how this Hot Springs water will put lead in your pencil. Pretty soon the Yankee says, "Boys, I can feel my cork a-bobbing already!" So then he put on his clothes and run down the road to a whore-house, and he says the water here sure is wonderful.

It was pretty near daylight when the policeman come along. There was a little boy setting on the front step, and he was a-crying. "What's the matter, Bub?" says the policeman. "My mommy is dead," says the little boy, "and them two fancy women that stayed with us is dead, too." The policeman figured maybe the boy just had a nightmare, so he asked him what killed all them women. "It was a hard-peckered Yankee with whiskers," says the little boy, "that come in here and fucked 'em to death." The policeman walked into the house, and there laid three whores dead as a door-nail.

"Good Lord," says he, "I have been around Hot Springs for a long time, but I never seen nothing like this before!"

So pretty soon the policeman says, "Where did this hard-peckered Yankee go?" The little boy was still a-crying. "He's out in the south pasture, a-chasing our heifers," says the little boy.

They used to tell lots of stories like that, about the water in the Old Ral Hole. Probably it is just a pack of lies. But there ain't no denying that some mighty peculiar things happened around them bath-houses at Hot Springs.

[X735.8.1.1]
Randolph prefaces this story with the following explanation: "Neuralgia was once a euphemism for syphilis; in the advanced stages the humorists called it old-ralgia, shortened to *old ral* (Dacus and Buel, *A Tour of St. Louis,* pp. 354–355). A ramshackle building at Hot Springs known as the 'Old Ral Hole' was described as 'a place where syphilitic paupers could bathe in the curative waters without charge' (Clugston, *Facts You Should Know About Arkansas,* p. 23). The natives have always contended that the Hot Springs water is aphrodisiac." Interestingly, in another of his manuscript collections, "Bawdy Elements in Ozark Speech," p. 66, Randolph gives an item stating that Hot Springs water is overrated as an aphrodisiac.

Ernest Baughman reported that he had heard a tale similar to this one in Indiana in 1929. Lockridge, *Waggish Tales,* pp. 122–127, presents a variant, in which a man takes a week's supply of aphrodisiac pills in one day, with fatal results to the female members of his family.

58. Guns under the Pillow

Told by Ed Halley, Aurora, Mo., September, 1934.

One time there was a young doctor that got benighted away out in the hills, because his automobile broke down. He come to a house where two sisters was a-living all alone. The girls didn't want to keep him at first, but there wasn't no other place that he could go, and it was a-raining besides, so finally they says all right. The house didn't have only one room, but there was three beds in it.

The oldest girl says, "Doc, me and Sis don't want no foolishness here," and she showed him a big six-shooter that was under her pillow. Then the youngest girl says, "That's right," and she had a big six-shooter under her pillow, too. Both of 'em says the doctor will have to stay in his own bed and behave himself, or else they would blow his guts out. "All right, ladies," says the doctor, "I will do just as you say."

Along in the night the oldest sister begun to mumble something, like she was a-talking in her sleep. "My gun ain't loaded," she says, "my gun ain't loaded." The doctor was feeling kind of horny, so he crawled over there, and they sure did have a good time. Then he slipped back to his own bed and went to sleep.

After while he woke up again, and this time the youngest sister was a-mumbling. "My gun ain't loaded," she says, "my gun ain't loaded." So pretty soon the doctor crawled over there and topped her. She was better frigging than the other girl, so he diddled her twice. Then he slipped back to his own bed and went to sleep.

The next time Doc woke up, the girls was a-talking in their sleep again, and both of 'em says, "My gun ain't loaded, my gun ain't loaded." But this time the young doctor just laid there. "You'll have to excuse me, ladies," says he, "because my gun ain't loaded, either!"

All three of em just laughed like fools, and pretty soon they went back to sleep. Next morning the girls fixed Doc a fine big breakfast, and the oldest one says he can sleep in their house any time he wants to, no matter if his gun is loaded or not.

[X735.9.1]

Randolph notes a similar tale in Lockridge, *Waggish Tales,* pp. 111–114, involving three women. In Hall, *Anecdota,* II, No. 283, it is a woman who has the unloaded pistol to protect the virtue of her two daughters. Legman, *Rationale,* I, 354, offers one from *Memorabilia* (1910) in which the mountaineer holds the pistol to protect his wife and sister-in-law. He further gives a variant form, collected in Washington, D.C., in 1943, in which the father holds an apparently loaded shotgun to protect his nine daughters from the traveling salesman. By the time the fifth one makes his request, threatening to tell her father unless the salesman complies, the traveler says that he'd rather be shot than fucked to death.

59. The Two Old Men

Told by Ed Wall, Pineville, Mo., August, 1929. He had the story from a man named Kolley, who lived near Cyclone, Mo., in the 1890's.

One time there was a king that was very rich, but somebody broke in at night and run off with a lot of his gold. The king got up early and seen the stuff was gone, but nobody knowed who done it. There was two old men that lived right close, and the folks figured them old men must have stole the king's treasure.

When they come to the first old man's house, he was asleep in bed. The soldiers woke him up, but he says, "I hit the hay early, and slept sound all night, until right this minute." The old man got out of bed, and the king watched him for a long time. "I'm eighty years old, and my time is short," says the old man. "I ain't interested in things like gold, because my mind is set on treasures laid up in Heaven." So then the king and the soldiers walked out.

When they come to the second old man's house, he was asleep in bed. Soon as the soldiers woke him up, he says "Excuse me, I got to take a piss," and he went outside. And the king says, "Did you sleep sound all night?" The old man says "Well, maybe I got up once or twice." So then the king and the soldiers walked out.

"The first old man done it," says the king, "the one that has got his mind on Heaven." The soldiers begun to dig, and pretty soon they found the gold in the first old man's garden. So then somebody asked the king how he could tell which one was the thief. "An old man has got to piss, when he first gets up," says the king. "I watched that fellow quite awhile, but he didn't piss, so I knowed he hadn't been in bed long."

The folks begun to talk about what a smart man the king is, but he says brains don't amount to much, because it depends mostly on kidneys and bladder. "I understand about things like that, because I'm pretty near eighty myself," says the king.

[J1661.1.10.1]
Thompson, *Motif-Index* (J1661.1), gives an extensive listing of tales based on the motif of clever deductions from observation. In 1959 I collected a story similar to Randolph's from an old wood hick, Hiram Cranmer, of Hammersley Fork, Penna. Cranmer said that he had seen it "in an old book of stories" about 1910.

60. Twelve-Dollar Jack

Told by J. C. Short, Galena, Mo., October, 1939. Mr. Short heard it about 1899, related as a true story.

One time there was some fellows hanging around the store, and they got to talking about which one had the longest tool. So finally Jim Henson laid eight silver dollars in a row on the counter. Then he out with his old jemson, and it sure was a dandy. He brushed seven of them silver dollars off onto the floor. The eighth dollar moved a little bit, but Jim's pecker wasn't quite long enough to knock it off'n the table.

Then old Harmon Kenny stepped forward and done the same thing, only he brushed *ten* silver dollars off onto the floor. "I don't never do no bragging about things like that," says Harmon, "but I will bet twenty-five dollars. If there is any man in this town can do better, let him put up or shut up."

Pretty soon there was a big fellow spoke up, and his name was John E. Brown, but everybody called him Jack. "Does whickerbills count?" says he. The boys argued awhile, but there ain't no denying that a whickerbill is part of a man's prick, so finally Harmon Kenny says yes. Well sir, Jack pulled out the God-awfullest tool you ever seen, only on a jackass. And when he drawed his whickerbill forward it made the thing about three inches longer. "Line up your money," says Jack Brown, and then he swung around and raked *twelve* silver dollars off'n the table.

Harmon Kenny handed over the money without no argument, and John E. Brown was knowed as Twelve-Dollar Jack from that day forward. There was some foreigners tried to get him to travel with a side-show, but Twelve-Dollar Jack just laughed in their face. "It is kind of vulgar for a man to go around showing his pecker to strangers," says he, "and therefore I don't want no part of it."

[X712.2.1.3]
Randolph notes that "whickerbill" is the Ozark word for prepuce (Randolph and Wilson, *Down in the Holler*, p. 298). He also refers to Richard M. Dorson's tale of "Horsecock Charlie, who would exhibit his oversized organ for twenty-five cents, and who met his death when, asleep in an upper bunk, his outsized member fell over the side and the weight pulled poor Charlie crashing to the floor" (*JAF*, LXIV, 234). An almost exact parallel

to Randolph's tale appears in [White?], *The Bagnio Miscellany,* p. 74.

61. They Couldn't Learn Him Nothing

Told by Fred High, Berryville, Ark., October, 1953. It was a familiar story in Berryville, he says, about 1900.

One time there was an old farmer that had three grown girls. And then a big country boy came along, but he didn't have much sense, as he was kind of a half-wit. The big country boy hadn't never done no fucking, but he wants somebody to show him how, so he can court a rich man's daughter that lives in town.

The oldest girl says, "Anybody can do it easy, and you just come with me." So they went in the hayloft, and she says, "Throw me down." The big country boy throwed her clear out of the barn, and it pretty near killed her. "I can't learn that fool nothing," says the oldest girl, and she gives up the whole thing right there.

The middle-sized girl just laughed, and she say, "You let me try him once." So they went in the weaving-shed, and she pulled her dress away up high. "Jam it to me!" she says. But the big country boy hauled off and hit her with his fist, because he thought that was what she meant, and it pretty near knocked her senseless. So she give up and quit right there. "I can't learn that fool nothing," says the middle-sized girl.

The youngest girl says, "You watch me handle him." They went in the kitchen, and she pulled off all her clothes. "Just lay me down easy," says she, and he done it. "Now stick the horn in me," she says. The big country boy grabbed the dinner horn that was hanging on a nail, but the tooting end of the horn was too big, and it pretty near ruined her. "I can't learn that fool nothing," says the youngest girl, and she give up the whole thing right there.

The big country boy went to town and married the rich man's daughter, anyhow. Everybody figured they wouldn't do no good, but him and her got along fine. The folks never did find out what happened, but the rich man's daughter just laughed, because she knowed more about fucking than them cornfed country girls ever heard tell of.

[X732.1.2]
Variants of the motif of the boy who is ignorant of sexual intercourse are widespread. One of these, collected in France (*Kryptadia*, II, 15–17), has the foolish bridegroom instructed to mount his wife and push where he finds hair. He mounts crossways and gets nowhere. In Afanasiev, *Stories*, pp. 20–24, the groom misunderstands instructions and spends the wedding night hanging on the wall instead of in bed with his bride.

The inability of the country girls to teach the boy anything about sex, and the subsequent apparent success of the city girl, is a reversal of the usual roles in rural humor. Ordinarily the city girl, for all her sophisticated airs, is shown up as having little real knowledge of down-to-earth sex. See Number 92 of this collection, "The City Girl and the Cow," or compare the sequence in the 1956 motion picture, "Bus Stop," in which Virgil explains to Cherie (Marilyn Monroe) that Bo was raised way out in the country and never had anything to do with girls. Cherie answers that she's from the country, too, and has been kissing boys since she was knee-high to a . . .

62. Tom Burdick's Pecker

Told by Lon Jordan, Farmington, Ark., November, 1941.
He heard it near Fayetteville, Ark., about 1903.

One time there was a fellow named Tom Burdick that fucked pretty near every woman on the creek, and so after awhile his health broke down. Finally old Tom died, and the neighbors come over to lay out the corpse, because there wasn't no undertakers in them days. Tom Burdick's body was laying in a pine box, but his pecker stuck up like a fence-post. Hard as a rock, too, and it stood so tall they couldn't put the lid on the coffin.

The folks never seen a corpse act like that before, and they figured Tom's pecker would crumple soon as the evening sun went down. But the goddam thing just stood there, and seemed like it was getting harder all the time. So finally Sis Hopper went and told the widow. Old lady Burdick come in the parlor where they had Tom laid out, and she seen how things was. "What do you want we should do about it?" says one of the granny-women.

The widow-woman just stared at old Burdick's pecker. "For all I care," says she, "you can cut the thing off and stick it up his ass." The folks was all surprised to hear such talk about her own husband. "Surely, you don't mean that!" says Sis Hopper, which everybody knowed she had laid up with Tom Burdick herself, whenever they got a chance. The widow Burdick looked at Sis mighty hard. "Why not?" she says. "Even when he was alive, Tom wasn't none too particular where he put it."

Poor Sis Hopper never said another word, and the widow-woman walked out of the room like she didn't have a care in the world. Them people never did tell what happened after that. But everybody could see that the coffin-lid was screwed down tight when they buried Tom Burdick next morning.

[X712.2.2.1]

Legman, *Rationale,* I, 346, 655–657, relates a similar story collected in California in 1936, and again in New York in 1948, with the addition of an unsuccessful attempt to masturbate the penis down. He also notes a tale in Louis Perceau, *Histoire d'Hommes et de Dames* (1913), p. 99, in which a man dies in the midst of a sexual orgy brought on by an aphrodisiac; his corpse must be masturbated three times before the top can be put on the coffin.

63. What Madeline Done

Told by J. E. Dunwoody, Clinton, Iowa, March, 1951. He heard it in McDonald County, Mo., about 1900.

One time there was a woman named Madeline that showed up missing, and nobody knowed what become of her. Somebody seen her in the Antlers Hotel, and maybe she run off with old Colonel Baker, because the colonel is pretty well fixed. But when Madeline's sister heard about it, she begun to holler that somebody must have murdered Madeline, and hid the corpse. She wanted the sheriff to arrest Colonel Baker, but the sheriff won't do it because they haven't got no evidence. And nobody knowed where the colonel is at, anyhow.

Madeline's sister believed in spirits, and she says they are always a-rapping on tables. Sometimes a table will raise right up off'n the floor, even if a fellow that weighed two hundred pounds is trying to hold it down. So Madeline's sister rented a room at the same hotel, and there was a writing table in it. She got some other people that believe in spirits, and the whole bunch set down with their hands on the table. They kept asking the spirits what has become of Madeline, but there wasn't no answer for a long time.

Finally they could feel the table move a little. Somebody says, "Is Madeline dead?" and the table give a loud rap that means "No." Then Madeline's sister says, "Was she in this hotel?" and the table give two loud raps which means "Yes." Pretty soon Madeline's sister says, "Was she here with Colonel Baker?" The table jumped a foot high, and give two raps the loudest you ever heard. So then she says, "What did Madeline do?" The table just flopped plumb over so its legs was sticking up, and the drawers flew open!

The fellow that works on the newspaper laughed like a fool. The rest of them people just set there goggle-eyed for a minute, and then they got up and went home. The story don't say what happened after that.

[X749.3.1]

Legman, *Rationale*, II, 217, relates a similar story without noting his source. In this instance, the departed spirit of an actress proves her identity by having the table act in the same manner. In addition to commenting on the character of Madeline, one cannot help but feel that the story is also intended to poke fun at the Spiritualist movement, which was widely popular during the latter part of the nineteenth century.

64. The Cold-Blooded Husband

Told by Gene Carter, Eureka Springs, Ark., September, 1953.

One time there was a young couple got married, and the first night the young fellow didn't give his wife no attention at all. He just laid there a-reading magazines till way late, then he blowed out the light and went to sleep. The bride was terrible disappointed, but she didn't say nothing. When they went to bed the second night it was just the same thing over again, but the girl never made no complaint.

She told her mother about it next day, but the old lady says for her not to worry, because everything will work out all right. "Maybe he's one of them fellows that don't like a fancy nightgown," she says. Next time, you take off every stitch except your best stockings, and wear them fine red garters." The girl done just like she said, and the old lady was peeking through the keyhole. Pretty soon she could see the young fellow's hand reach over and touch the girl's twitchet. Soon as she seen that, the old lady figured everything was all right, so she went to bed and thought no more about it.

Next morning the girl was feeling mighty low, and she says that taking off her night-dress didn't do no good, because the young fellow just laid there a-reading his magazines. The old woman laughed. "Don't tell me that, honey," she says. "I was peeking through the keyhole, and I seen his hand reach over and touch your twitchet." But the girl just shook her head. "That don't mean nothing," says she. "He was just a-wetting his finger, to turn the goddam pages."

[X735.2.2]
Ernest Baughman reported to Randolph having heard this in Albuquerque in 1952. Hall, *Anecdota*, I, No. 217, gives the same story in the context of a tiff between the husband and wife. Another variant in the same collection, No. 352, contains the bashful bridegroom motif. The mother of the frustrated bride suggests to her daughter that she put her husband's hand on her pussy. The next morning the bride is more dismayed than ever; she had followed her mother's suggestion, and her husband got up and washed his hands.

65. Cats Don't Take No Chances

Told by Milton N. Cowell, Noel, Mo., August, 1928. We heard it on the Oklahoma frontier in the 1870's.

One time there was a city fellow come to see an old couple that lived away back in the timber. Him and the old man set

97

in the house and talked awhile. The old woman washed up the dishes, and there was three cats a-laying on the floor. It looked like they was sound asleep, but you can't never tell about cats.

All of a sudden the old man let a fart, and it was a pretty loud one. The old woman never turned a hair. But them three cats jumped up and took off like they was shot out of a gun. The city fellow looked kind of surprised. "What's the matter, stranger?" says the old man. "Nothing is the matter," says the city fellow. "I just was wondering what made them three cats run out of the door so quick."

The old man just laughed. "Them cats don't take no chances," he says. "My old woman is so deef she can't hear it thunder, but she's got a nose like a bird-dog. And every time she smells shit, she kicks hell out of the cats."

[X716.6.3]
I have not found any parallels to this little story of the perceptive cats. Hall, *Anecdota*, I, No. 116, is, perhaps, a related aphorism: "God put the stink in a fart for guys who are hard of hearing."

66. The Miller's Prick

Told by Ed Wall, Pineville, Mo., May, 1922. It was "just a made-up tale," he said, popular in the 1890's.

One time there was a miller married a girl that wasn't but twelve years old. He says it is better to pick 'em young, because a little girl don't know nothing about men, and she will believe anything you tell her. Soon as they got home from the preacher's home, the miller pulled out his prick. "Ain't that a dandy?" says he. "It's the only one in this county!" And then him and her went to bed, and she says married life sure is wonderful.

It was about a week after that when the miller's wife seen the postmaster out behind the office, and he was taking a piss. So that night she says, "Honey, the postmaster's got one of them things!" The miller just laughed. "Yes, says he, "I had two of 'em, and the postmaster is a good fellow, so I give him my spare." The girl just looked kind of big-eyed, and he laughed louder than ever.

The miller didn't hire no help, so mostly he was all tired out by night. There ain't nothing that will slow up a man's family duties like working ten hours in a grist-mill. Lots of times he would just eat his supper and then go to bed, and not do no fucking at all. The miller's wife never made no complaint. She just went down to the post office every day, after the ten o'clock mail was up. Her and the postmaster got to be pretty good friends.

One Sunday the miller stayed in bed late, because the mill was shut down, so he topped her three times before breakfast. And then he just laid there a-laughing, and he says, "A woman is mighty lucky to marry a man with a fine big tally-whacker like I got!" The miller's wife just giggled. "That's right," she says, "but I believe you give away the best one."

The girl looked kind of scared for a minute, after she said that. But the miller didn't pay no attention, because he figured whatever she says is nothing but childish prattle. He just kept on a-bragging about his prick. Well, what a man don't know ain't going to hurt him, and the miller's wife seen there wasn't no harm done. So pretty soon she cooked up a fine big Sunday breakfast, and him and her lived happy ever after.

[X712.4.3]

Randolph notes that he collected similar stories at Sallisaw, Okla., in 1934; at Springfield, Mo., in 1941; and at Eureka Springs, Ark., in 1948. Ernest Baughman told Randolph that he had heard it in Albuquerque in 1951. Hall, *Anecdota,* I, No. 71, gives it more specifically as a joke, with the wife seen coming out of the friend's house and telling her husband that he'd given away the best one. Legman, *Rationale*, I, 142, feels that the early form of the story is that given in Poggio, *Facetiae* (1451), No. 62, in which the husband pretends to have two penises but cannot produce the larger one when the unsatisfied wife asks for it. He also points out a variant in Béroalde de Verville, *Le Moyen de Parvenir* (1610), ch. 23, in which the unsatisfied wife gives the husband money to buy a better penis. She asks what he did with the old one, and he tells her he threw it away. She observes that he shouldn't have done that, for it would have been just right for her mother.

67. Let's Play Whammy!

Told by Edward E. Wagner, Eureka Springs, Ark., July, 1953. He got it from a native of Little Rock, Ark., in the 1940's.

One time there was a fellow named Brooks that lived on the second floor of the hotel. He took a few drinks at the tavern, and a girl come along that was drinking gin, so pretty soon him and her got to talking. But she says it looks kind of vulgar for people to set around in taverns, so they bought another bottle and went up to his room at the hotel.

After awhile he says, "Let's play whammy," but the girl never heard of whammy, and she says how do you do it? "We just take off our clothes," says he, "and you stand at one side of the room, while I stand on the other side. Then we run towards each other fast, and meet in the middle." The girl says that sounds like a fine game, and we will try it once. But they had got pretty drunk by that time, so Brooks missed the girl and fell out of the window.

The fellow didn't get hurt much because he had fell in

some bushes, but there wasn't no way to get back through the window because it is too high off the ground. So he went to the kitchen door, and told the porter to fetch him a raincoat or something. But the porter says there ain't no need of that. "Jesus Christ!" says Brooks, "you want me to walk through the hotel stark naked, with all them people a-looking at me?" The porter says it is all right, because nobody will see you.

So then he looked through the glass in the door, and sure enough the lobby was plumb empty, and nobody in the dining room neither. Brooks couldn't figure out what become of all the people, because it was only eight o'clock, so he asked the hotel clerk. "Oh, they're all upstairs," says the clerk, "a-watching the doctors trying to get some woman off of a doorknob."

[X735.5.2]
Legman, *Rationale*, II, 453–454, indicates having heard a very similar form of the story in New York in 1952. Buehler collected it for his master's thesis, pp. 57–58, from a native of Kokomo, Ind. He also notes a version of it in Elgart, *Still More Over Sexteen*, pp. 88–89. In Elgart's version, as in Randolph's, the man goes out the window and is concerned about getting back to his room without being seen. In Buehler's, he "racks up his balls" on the bedpost; as he lies there moaning, his wife asks him to get her off the doorknob.

68. Follow Your Leader

Told by Ross Coleman, Eureka Springs, Ark., July, 1950. It was a common story around Green Forest, Ark., in the 1930's.

One time there was a farmer that give his boy hell, because the young fellow would go to town pretty near every night.

"Pappy," says the boy, "you're just jealous because you have got old, and can't do no running around yourself." But Pappy says it is foolish to talk like that. "We'll both go to town," says he. "You just follow me, and do everything I do. I reckon that will show who's the best man!" So the young fellow says all right.

Soon as they got to town the old man tossed off a whole bottle of whiskey, with a horse-quart of beer for a chaser. The boy done his best, but he couldn't drink that much liquor. Next they went to the hotel, and the old man eat the biggest beefsteak you ever seen, with three orders of fried potatoes. The boy done pretty good, but he couldn't eat no such a bait as that. Finally the old man headed for the whore-house, and the boy says to himself "Here is one place I will beat the old booger easy, no matter what he does!"

When they got in the whore-house the old man started kidding the girls and giving them some money. Pretty soon he had four of 'em a-prancing around the room stark naked, while him and the young fellow just watched 'em. Finally the old man pulled out his big long tallywhacker, and tied it in a knot. "All right, son," says he. "Let's see you do that!"

The boy just set there goggle-eyed, because he couldn't even bend his pecker, no matter if his life depends on it. So pretty soon they both went back home, and that is the end of the story. It just goes to show that one man's meat is another man's poison, as the fellow says.

[F547.3.7]
Ernest Baughman reported having heard a similar tale about a Texan who wrapped it three times around his finger. He heard the tale in New Mexico, but his informant got it in Oklahoma. Buehler, in his master's thesis, pp. 118–120, has a variant form of the story from an Indiana informant, in which a boy challenges a Cadillac salesman, with a new car as the stakes. He undresses and feels up his sleeping eighteen-year-old sister, then takes out

his penis and wraps it around his finger, asking the salesman if he can do that. The salesman asks him what color car he wants.

69. Senator Johnson's Great Speech

Told by H. A. Converse, Little Rock, Ark., December, 1949. He had a manuscript copy of the speech, but recited the whole thing from memory.

One time there was a goddam Yankee moved to Arkansas, and got elected to the Legislature. The first thing he done was put in a bill to make Arkansas rhyme with Kansas, just because it is spelled that way. The Arkansawyers got pretty mad, of course, so they begun to stomp and holler. There was one old man that hollered louder than anybody else, and finally the rest of 'em quietened down to hear what he had to say.

"Mr. Speaker, God damn your soul," says he, "I've been trying to get the floor for thirty minutes, but all you do is squirm around like a dog with a flea in his ass! I'm Senator Cassius F. Johnson from Johnson County, where we raise men with peckers on, and the women are glad of it. Why, gentlemen, at the tender age of sixteen them girls can throw their left tit over their right shoulder, and squirt milk up their ass-hole as the occasion demands! When I was fourteen years old my prick was big as a roasting-ear, the pride and joy of the whole goddam settlement. Gentlemen, I could piss half-way across the Ouachita!"

Everybody clapped when they heard that, but the Speaker begun to holler "Out of order! Out of order!" and pound on his desk.

"You're goddam right it was out of order," says Senator

Johnson, "otherwise I could have pissed clear across the son-of-a-bitch! That's the kind of folks we raise in Johnson County, gentlemen, and we ain't never been dictated to by nobody. And now comes this pusillanimous blue-bellied Yankee who wants to change the name of Arkansas. Why, Mister Speaker, he compares the great state of Arkansas to *Kansas!* You might as well liken the noonday sun in all its glory to the feeble glow of a lightning-bug's ass, or the fragrance of an American Beauty rose to the foul quintessence of a Mexican burro's fart! Can all the power of this Assembly enlargen the puny penis of a Peruvian prince to a ponderous Pagan prick, or the tiny testicles of a Turkish tyrant to the bulky bollyz of a Roman gladiator? Change the name of Arkansas? Great God Almighty damn! No, gentlemen! Hell fire, no!

"What the God damn hell is things a-coming to, anyhow? Why, gentlemen, it's got so a man can't take down his pants for a good country shit without getting his ass full of bird-shot. Change the name of Arkansas? Great God Almighty damn! You may piss on Jefferson's grave, gentlemen. You may shit down the White House steps, and use the Declaration of Independence for a corncob. You may rape the Goddess of Liberty at high noon, and wipe your tallywhacker on the Star Spangled Banner. You may do all this, gentlemen, and more. But you can't change the name of Arkansas! Not while one patriot lives to prevent such desecration! Change the name of Arkansas? Hell fire, no!"

History don't tell us what happened after that, but everybody knows the Yankee's bill was killed, dead as a whore's turd in a piss-pot. Them son-of-a-bitches up North think the whole thing was just a joke, and some of 'em claim Senator Johnson didn't make no speech at all. But every true-blooded Arkansawyer knows that Senator Cassius M. Johnson jumped into the breech that day, to save the Bear State from treason and disgrace. We ain't going to forget it, neither.

Randolph's own documentation of this piece is excellent. He observes that the controversy about the pronunciation of Arkansas is discussed, with rich documentation by Allen Walker Read (*American Speech*, VIII, 42–46). There is no official record of a senator named Cassius M. Johnson, or any evidence that such a speech was ever made in the Arkansas Legislature. It has been delivered at private parties, in bars and bawdy houses all over the country. Watered-down versions have been printed by Allsopp (*Folklore of Romantic Arkansas*, II, 87–89), Travis Y. Oliver (*Vanity Fair*, XLI [September, 1933], 57), Norwood (*Just a Book*, pp. 26–27), and many others. Masterson (*Tall Tales of Arkansas*, pp. 180–185, 352–354) devotes an entire chapter to this oration and prints several unexpurgated, fully documented texts.

Legman, *Rationale*, II, 755–758, presents an extensive discussion of the story, pointing out that such mock parliamentarian speeches are an outgrowth of the liberties allowed in the Saturnalia, and that prototypes of this kind of speech existed at least as far back as the early sixteenth century. He further observes that one of Masterson's texts, almost identical to that from Randolph's informant, had been sent to him by a relative of Mark Twain; he conjectures that the piece might have been written by Twain as a bit of satire when the pronunciation of the state name was formally established by the Arkansas Legislature in 1881.

The speech also has been recorded on an unlabeled, unnumbered 78 rpm disc, issued and sold "under the counter" in the late 1940's.

70. How God Made the Eastons

Told by Elbert Short, Crane, Mo., June, 1933. He regarded it as a true account of something that happened near Crane about 1915.

One time there was a fellow named Garvin that got along pretty good till he married one of the Easton girls. The

Eastons was a trashy lot, and from then on Garvin didn't have nothing but grief. Whenever one of the Easton boys would steal a cow, or get some girl knocked up, or run in debt at the store, poor old Garvin had to make it good. If he didn't, his wife would raise hell at home till it was enough to run a man crazy.

After awhile the biggest Easton boy joined the church, and pretty soon he got to preaching up on Candor Mountain. The sermon was about how God made man, and stirred up considerable argument. Because in the first chapter of the Book it says that God created men and women in His own image, but the second chapter tells how He made Adam out of dust. The fellows in the barbershop got to talking about it, and they argued pretty near all day. Pretty soon old Garvin come in to get his hair cut, and he heard them boys a-trying to quote Scripture.

Finally one of them Coon Creek fellows says, "Well, there ain't no doubt but what God made men and women, but the Book don't tell just how He done it. I reckon there was arms and legs and heads and all kinds of pieces, but the Old Master stuck 'em together kind of hasty, so that's why we ain't none of us perfect."

Most of the boys just shook their head, because they don't believe nothing like that, but Garvin says it seems reasonable to him. "When God got the job done," says he, "there was a big pile of ass-holes left over. It looks to me like the Almighty just throwed all them ass-holes together, and made the Easton family." Probably a town fellow would think that was foolish. But it sounds pretty sensible to anybody that knowed the Eastons, and seen them walking around with their mouth a-hanging open.

[X715.1]

As Randolph's informant seems to imply, this may be a local anecdote. There are many insulting jokes about in-laws, but I have not found any that directly parallel this one.

71. The Brag Heifer

Told by Mrs. Nina May Blake, Kansas City, Mo., April, 1929. She heard it near Poplar Bluff, Mo., about 1910.

One time there was an old man let a city fellow hunt on his farm, and the fellow killed a deer in some thick brush. But when he run up with knife, it wasn't no deer at all, but a slick little Jersey heifer. The hunter was an honest man, so he went back to the house and told the farmer how it happened. "I'll pay whatever is right," says he, and pulled out his wallet.

The old farmer begun to holler like hell, with big tears a-running down his face. "Good God," says he, "that was my brag heifer, which I wouldn't have took no amount of money for her. Why, she had a cunt just like a woman!" The town fellow kind of brightened up when he heard that. "Don't you worry, old-timer," says he. "I'll fetch my wife out here tomorrow. You and her ought to get along fine, because she's got a cunt just like a cow!"

[X712.1.3.1]

A variant form appears in Hall, *Anecdota*, II, No. 241, in which a farmer at a fair sees a cow that's worth a million dollars because it has a pussy like a woman's. He bursts out laughing, and observes that his wife has a pussy like a cow's, but it isn't worth a nickel. Related stories in which there is direct insult about the large vagina are widespread. Another in *Anecdota*, II, No. 302, has the girl defecate over a cliff above a lake. She remarks to her boyfriend that she did it into a canoe below. He informs her that it was no canoe, but the reflection of her cunt. In *Kryptadia*, II, 154–155 (from France), a woman bends over and asks her young daughter to apply medication from a syringe. The child says that if she means the lower hole, she could pour it in from a bucket. In another of the Randolph manuscript collections, "Bawdy Elements in Ozark Speech," p. 25, a girl, exasperated by a man continually peering up her skirt, finally raises it up and asks if he never saw one before. He replies that he has, but never one that looked like he could get back into it.

72. The Speckle-Ass Bull

Told by Frank Shelton, Fayetteville, Ark., May, 1952. He heard the story in Yell County, Ark., about 1932.

One time there was a fool country boy that owned a little bull, with some spots on its hind end. The boy says the bull's name is Speckle-Ass. The folks thought this was comical, so they all got to calling it Speckle-Ass too, when there wasn't no strangers around. Things like that was kind of a neighborhood joke, in them days.

The funny thing happened when somebody left the gate open, so the little bull got loose and run off. That fool boy went all over the country, asking people if anybody had saw his Speckle-Ass bull. The folks all laughed when he said that, so they would give the boy a good dinner, and then send him on to the next farm.

Pretty soon there was a young couple come along in a fine buggy, but the fool country boy hid in the brush because he didn't like town people. The girl got out and went behind some bushes to piss. She told her boy-friend not to peek, but the young fellow done it anyhow, and he says "My God, I see the world and all that's in it!" The fool country boy come a-tearing out of the brush when he heard that. "Listen, Mister," says he, "did you see my Speckle-Ass bull?"

The young fellow didn't return no answer, but the girl run back to the buggy, and they took off in a cloud of dust. Nobody knows what them town people thought, but the home folks all got a good laugh out of it.

Aarne-Thompson, *Type Index*, gives this tale as Type 1355B, "Adulteress Tells Her Lover, 'I Can See the Whole World.'" In its earliest known form, it appears in the fifteenth-century *One Hundred Merrie and Delightsome Stories* (ed. de la Sale), No. 12. Legman, *Rationale*, I, 381, points out an updated form, with an absent-minded professor searching for his umbrella, which was heard in New York in 1940 and appeared in several college humor magazines in the 1940's, as well as a still later version, with a World War II barracks bag as the object of the search, heard in 1953.

73. Something on a Stump

Told by Otho Pratt, Verona, Mo., April, 1951. A true account, he says, of something that happened in Stone County, Mo., about 1912.

One time there was a woman named Mattson that run a boarding house, and she got a country girl to wait on the table. Callie had been raised up on Sowcoon Mountain, and she thought it was terrible how the town girls laid up with the boys. "There ain't enough money in the world to make *me* carry on like that," says Callie. "Why, I'd rather stretch my cunt over a stump, and let the crows pick it!" Old Lady Mattson told her husband what Callie said, and it tickled him so he had to tell some of the men that stayed at the boarding house.

Next day old lady Mattson and Callie had dinner ready at twelve o'clock, but the boarders wasn't there. And pretty soon they all come a-marching in together. So then the old lady asked somebody how come they was fifteen minutes late? The boarders just set still and looked solemn, till finally old Judge McKay spoke up. "Ma'm," says he, "there was a big flock of crows down by the river, a-pecking at something stretched on a stump. We all went down there, to see what it was."

The old lady's eyes popped for a minute, and she had to bite her lip to keep from laughing. Callie just stood there with her mouth open, then she spun around and took out for the kitchen. She didn't stop at the back door neither, so old lady Mattson had to wait on the table herself. After the boarders was gone the womenfolks found Callie setting under a tree, and her face was red as a beet. "There ain't no decent people in this town," she says, "and I am going back to Sowcoon Mountain."

That's just what Callie done, too, and she told everybody that the boarders made fun of her twitchet right at the dinner table. So old lady Mattson got a girl from Horse Creek to help in the boarding house. Them Horse Creek girls are kind of used to town folks' ways, and they ain't so easy insulted.

[X60.1]
This belongs under what Thompson, *Motif-Index* (X1–X99), classifies as "Humor of Discomforture." I have found no parallel versions of this anecdote.

74. Have You Ever Been Diddled?

Told by J. L. Russell, Harrison, Ark., April, 1950. He heard this one near Berryville, Ark., in the 1890's.

One time there was a town girl and a country girl got to talking about the boys they had went with. The town girl told what kind of a car her boyfriends used to drive, and how much money their folks has got. But the country girl didn't take no interest in things like that, and she says the fellows are always trying to get into her pants.

So finally the town girl says, "Have you ever been diddled?" The country girl giggled, and she says yes, a little bit. "How much?" says the town girl. "Oh, about like that," says the country girl, and she held up her finger to show an inch, or maybe an inch and a half.

The town girl just laughed, and pretty soon the country girl says, "Have *you* ever been diddled?" The town girl says of course she has, lots of times. "How much?" says the country girl. "Oh, about like that," says the town girl, and she marked off about eight inches, or maybe nine.

The country girl just set there goggle-eyed, and she drawed a deep breath. "My God," says the country girl, "that ain't diddling! Why, you've been *fucked!*"

[J1805.5]
The humor in this story comes out of the different definitions applied to the word "diddle." In this respect, it is related to Number 49 of this collection, "It Was a Tee-Hee."

75. The Little End of Nothing

Told by H. F. Walker, Joplin, Mo., September, 1923. He got it from a "hillbilly" family in eastern Oklahoma.

One time there was a fresh-married couple lived up on Lightning Creek, but pretty soon the woman begun to holler for a divorce. Them people belong to the New Ground religion, and they was married in the church without no papers from the courthouse, so the law ain't got nothing to do with it. If anybody wants a divorce, they got to have a regular church trial.

When the preacher asked her what was the matter, the woman says her husband ain't no good. "That man's prick," she says, "is smaller than the little end of nothing, whittled down to a point!" The church folks decided to make the fellow stick his tallywhacker through a hole in the wall, where the members could walk past and look at it. Then they would all pray for guidance, and vote to see whether the woman got a divorce or not.

The woman's husband hired old Deacon Hodgepeth to stand behind the wall instead of him, because the deacon had a tool pretty near a foot long. The members come a-marching past, but they couldn't see where the woman has got no kick coming. Most of the womenfolks says, "That hussy ought to thank God every day!" and the rest of 'em hollered "Amen!" They sure wasn't going to give her no divorce, till old lady Witherspoon began to giggle. "Can't fool me," she says, "that's old Deacon Hodgepeth's pecker!"

The members all begun to holler when they heard that, and drug the deacon out from behind the partition. It was the darndest trial you ever seen. The woman got a divorce, all right. They withdrawed fellowship from her short-peckered husband, and old Deacon Hodgepeth too. Them New Ground preachers says that divorce is a mighty serious matter in the sight of God, and they won't stand for no fraud nor foolishness in the church house.

[K1919.2; X712.2.1.4]

Randolph points out that some backwoods cultists prefer extra-legal marriages, without any written record save a notation in the family Bible. He gives another tale, in which marriage and divorce is voted upon by the New Ground Church, in *Who Blowed Up the Church House?* pp. 65–67, 199.

The original of this tale goes back at least to the fifteenth-century *One Hundred Merrie and Delightsome Stories* (ed. de la Sale), No. 15. In one version from Scotland (*Kryptadia*, II,

261–262) the penis of the substituting minister is recognized by a female church member by the wart on the end of it. Legman, *Rationale*, I, 759, notes having heard the story in Orangeburg, N.Y., in 1944.

76. The Glory-Pole

Told by Bob Wyrick, Eureka Springs, Ark., November, 1950. It was one of many "preacher stories" that circulated near Green Forest, Ark., in the early 1900's.

One time there was a Holy Roller preacher walking through the woods, and he seen a pretty girl. "Sister, are you saved?" says he, and she told him yes. So then him and her walked along together, as they was going to a big meeting on Duck-butter Knob. The pretty girl kept a-talking about how fine it is to be a Christian, and what a wonderful blessing she has got already.

Pretty soon the preacher says, "I reckon you've seen the glory-pole," but the girl shook her head, because she never even heard of it. They set down on the ground, and the preacher pulled out his prick. "Is that the glory-pole?" she says, and run her hand over it. "That's the glory-pole," says he, "the axis of the world and the fount of all creation." The girl just looked at it admiring, and she says it sure is a dandy. "Just let me ease it into you," says the preacher, "and bring true salvation to your soul." The girl didn't return no answer, but she kept right on a-playing with the Reverend's pecker. So then he just give the pretty girl a good fucking, and she hollered "Praise God!" so loud you could hear it down to the big road.

They was late to the meeting, but she walked right in with the pine-straw still on her back. Pretty soon down come the Holy Spirit, so the pretty girl begun to wiggle her ass and holler. "Whoo-ee," she yelled, "there's blessings on my soul! Whoo-ee, he stuck the glory-pole up my piss-hole, and squirted salvation all over my ass-hole! Oh, praise God!"

The preacher was plumb flabbergasted for a minute, but the folks all hollered "Amen!" loud as they could, and kind of drowned her out. Lots of people lose their head when the Power gets a-hold of 'em, so they don't rightly know what they're a-saying. When anything like that happens in the church house, the folks just let on like they never heard it, and there ain't no harm done.

[X434.4]

This is clearly related to Aarne-Thompson Type 1425, "Putting the Devil into Hell." In France (*Kryptadia*, II, 128–129) it is called "Putting the Pope in Rome," and in another of Randolph's manuscript collections, "Vulgar Rhymes from the Ozarks," it becomes "Putting the Key to Heaven in the Lock." Randolph notes the use of the term "salvation pole" in the same context in Legman, *The Limerick*, p. 117, which Legman (*Rationale*, I, 417) identifies as having come from an American printed source of 1928.

77. Wind Instead of Water

Told by Mrs. Ethel R. Strainchamps, Springfield, Mo., June 1952. She heard it in Polk County, Mo., about 1924.

One time there was two travelers got lost away out in the Territory somewheres. It was one of them bad years, and there wasn't nothing to eat. They couldn't find a drop of water neither, and both of 'em was a-spitting cotton. Finally they come to a litle cabin on a hill. An old woman was a-setting on the porch, but the well had went dry and she didn't have a bite of victuals. It looked like all three of 'em has come to the end of their rope.

Pretty soon one of them fellows went a-rummaging round the smokehouse, and found an old flour sack. He seen a thin scattering of flour left in the seams, so they scraped it out careful into a sauce-dish. There wasn't only about three spoonfuls, but maybe enough to keep 'em alive another day. The hell of it is, you can't hardly eat flour dry like that, and they didn't have nothing to wet it down with.

So finally they says to the old woman it would be nice if you could piss a few drops on the flour, and maybe save all our lives. The old woman set the sauce-dish on the floor, and squatted down over it. The travelers just set there a-holding their breath, but it looks like the old woman couldn't pee a drop. She kept right on a-trying, though. Then all of a sudden she let a terrible big fart, and blowed all the flour away.

The story don't say what happened after that, because nobody ever did find out if the travelers starved to death or not. It's just one of them old tales that folks used to tell, in the early days.

[X716.7.1]
Legman, *Rationale*, II, 967–977, gives an almost identical story, heard in New York in 1938 and attributing the event to the ill-fated Donner Party, lost in the snow while searching for a pass through the mountains to California in the last century. There are, in addition, many related tales of disastrous or outrageous breaking wind. In Lockridge, *Waggish Tales*, pp. 257–260, a violinist breaks wind mightily just as he reaches the climax of an impressionistic piece about a storm. An enraptured girl interprets that section as lightning striking a privy. In another of his manuscript collections, " 'Unprintable' Songs from the Ozarks," Randolph has an item in which a wife and husband fight because he objects to her habit of breaking wind and de-

fecating in the haymow. On the other side of the coin, there are also tales of the more fortuitous breaking of wind, as in Afanasiev, *Stories,* pp. 6–7, and *Kryptadia,* II, 83–84 (from France).

78. First Time for Trudie

Told by Jeff Strong at Roaring River, near Cassville, Mo., April, 1941. He heard the story in Aurora, Mo., about 1910.

One time there was a girl named Trudie that had been a-screwing around town since she was twelve years old, and the respectable people wouldn't have nothing to do with her. But a big lawyer from Chicago come down here in the summertime, so all of a sudden him and Trudie got married. The home folks all let on like Trudie was the best girl that ever walked, because it always tickles them to see a Yankee get the worst of a bad bargain.

Everybody rallied round and give 'em a fine wedding, so the rich lawyer rented the best house in town, and throwed a big party. After it was over him and Trudie went to bed. The windows was all open, and some ornery town boys sneaked up to peek in. Just as the Yankee was a-mounting her, Trudie says "Honey, you've got your pecker where no man has ever been before." The boys didn't wait to hear no more.

When they got back to town, them boys was still laughing about where the rich man put his pecker, and one fellow says "reckon he must have stuck it up her ass!" That crack got to be kind of a by-word around here. Whenever anybody told a big lie, some fellow would say, "He must have stuck it up her ass!" Then everybody would laugh like hell, because it put 'em in mind of what Trudie told the rich Yankee that time.

[X722.2.1]
Randolph notes a similar tale in Lockridge, *Waggish Tales,*
pp. 176–180. Ernest Baughman reported having heard it in
Albuquerque in 1952, with the line, "He's got it in her ear." A
version more closely paralleling Randolph's may be found in
Hall, *Anecdota,* I, No. 230, which Legman, *Rationale,* I, 484,
traces back to the English erotic periodical *The Pearl,* No. 4,
October, 1879.

79. Cora and the Bottle

Told by a gentleman in Siloam Springs, Ark., April, 1930.

One time there was a wealthy family named Wilson that lived
in this county, and they had a pretty daughter about sixteen
years old. Lots of boys wanted to go with her, but Cora
wouldn't have nothing to do with them. She says they ain't
good enough for her, and the whole Wilson family acted like
they thought Cora's shit didn't stink.

It was a Saturday morning when old man Wilson come
a-riding into town, and he looked plumb worried. Pretty
soon Doc Holton got in his buggy, and followed the old man
home. Everybody seen Doc's rig a-standing in front of the
Wilson place pretty near all day. The word got around that
Cora had took sick, but nobody knowed what was the matter
with her.

After awhile the folks found out that Cora has been screwing herself with a beer bottle, and all of a sudden she couldn't
get the bottle out. It was the suction that done it. Cora got
scared, and begun to holler so loud she roused the whole
neighborhood. The womenfolks all pulled hard as they could,
but the bottle never budged. They was afraid to bust it for
fear the glass would cut Cora's cunt, and maybe she'd be

jill-flirted for life. So finally they had to send for the doctor.

When the Doc got there he says for them to drill a hole in the glass, because soon as you let in a little air the bottle will slip out easy. But the Wilson's didn't have no tools to bore a hole in glass. They tried files, and emery-dust, and the blacksmith's drill, and glass-cutters, and strings soaked in kerosene, and God knows what all. Finally the glass cracked on one side just a little bit, and then Doc pulled the bottle out slick as a whistle.

Soon as Cora got to feeling better, Doc Holton give her some good advice. Nobody ever did find out what Doc said, but pretty soon she married one of them long-peckered Bradley boys. Him and her never did get along very good. But it is better than sticking a beer-bottle up your cunt, anyhow.

[X712.1.1.2]

This would appear to be a widely known story through the Midwest. Ernest Baughman indicated that he heard it in Indiana numerous times, and Randolph states that he heard variants at a dozen other villages in Missouri, Arkansas, and Oklahoma, and that it is always given as a true story, with the name of some local girl. See Number 8 of this collection, "Billy Fraser Got Stuck," for a related story.

80. Wahoo! Wahoo!

Told by Ross Coleman, Eureka Springs, Ark., February, 1951.

One time there was a fellow that went over in the Creek Nation, and he mounted a likely young squaw that couldn't talk no English. She kept a-hollering "Wahoo! Wahoo!" but the fellow stayed right with her till he got his gun off twice.

That same day he went in the poolhall at Crooked Arrow, and it was full of Indians a-playing call-shot. Soon as one Indian would shoot, the rest of them hollered "Wahoo!" and then they would argue in Creek talk. The fellow got to thinking, so after awhile he asked one of them Indians about it. The Indian says "Well, if a man calls his shot in the side pocket, and then scratches it somewhere else, we all holler *wahoo* right quick, otherwise the son-of-a-bitch might say he was aiming for the other pocket all the time."

The fellow seen how it was, all right, just like little boys holler "Vents!" when they are playing marbles. But he was still thinking about that squaw. "Yeah," says he, "but what does the word *wahoo* mean, no matter if you're in the poolhall or not?" The Indian just looked at him. "That's what I been telling you. It don't mean nothing except *wrong hole*," says the Indian.

[X733.1.1]

Randolph cites an article by Maurice A. Mook, "North Pennsylvania Wellerisms," *JAF*, LXX, 183–184, in which Mook states that pool players in Crawford County, Penna., about 1915–35, used to say, "Wahoo, wahoo, said the Indian squaw," when the ball went into the wrong pocket of the pool table, and that everyone knew that " 'wahoo' meant 'wrong hole.' " Ernest Baughman informed Randolph that he had heard the story in Indiana in 1928. Hall, *Anecdota*, I, No. 439, gives a version close to Randolph's. Legman, *Rationale*, II, 165, also offers a version similar to Randolph's, collected in Idaho in 1919.

Randolph feels that perhaps this is related to the story about the Englishwoman who shouted, "Top-hole! Top-hole!" and the American sailor who replied, "That's where I've got it, lady." The original of this variant may be Hall, *Anecdota*, I, No. 343, in which the sailor, just in from a long voyage, rushes to the nearest brothel. He mounts the girl "dog fashion," but in his haste hits the wrong hole. When the girl complains, he answers, " 's all right, girlie, 's all right. Any port in a storm."

81. Senator Banks

Told by James Forsyth, Tulsa, Okla., January, 1937. He heard the story near Poplar Bluff, Mo., in the 1920's.

One time the boys was going to initiate some fellows into the Lodge. One of 'em was Senator Banks, and they locked him in a thing like a big bird-cage, only it was made out of heavy iron bars. Pretty soon a drunk man come walking down the aisle a-mumbling foolishness, so some of the brothers told him to set down and keep quiet. But the drunk sassed 'em right back. "Piss on you," says he.

The brothers begun to grumble, and they says, "Put that man out." But the drunk give a big jump, and got on top of Senator Banks's cage. "Piss on you," says he. And pretty soon he says, "By God, I *will* piss on you!" So then the drunk man pulled out his pecker and begun to wave it around like a fire-hose. Soon as the Senator felt the warm water a-falling on him, he roared like a bull, and shook the door of the cage. "Let me out, you son-of-a-bitches!" yelled the Senator. "To hell with your goddam Lodge!" The drunk man kept right on a-pissing, and the brothers couldn't stop him. Senator Banks was jumping up and down like a wild man, a-cussing the worst you ever heard. He says the brothers are all fools and the Lodge don't amount to a fart in a whirlwind, also he didn't want to join anyhow, but some drunken bum talked him into it. He says their charter ought to be took away by the Legislature, and he will sue every son-of-a-bitch in the Lodge if they don't get him out in two minutes.

About that time the drunk man jumped down off'n the cage. He wasn't drunk at all, only pretending like he was drunk, as he was one of the prize drill team from Saint Louis, but there was only a few of the brothers that knowed it. That big prick wasn't nothing but a rubber dummy, and the piss was just warm water out of a bottle under his coat.

Some of the brothers laughed when they seen it was just a joke. But Senator Banks says to hell with such jokes, and God damn anybody that ain't got no more sense, which they ought to be ashamed of theirself. The folks had to argue with Senator Banks a long time, before they could get him calmed down enough for the serious part of the initiation. Everybody says it is the funniest thing that ever happened in this town, but they never done no laughing while old Brother Banks was around.

[X717.2.1]

This would appear to be a local anecdote, but Legman's description of the rituals of the Order of the Beggar's Benison and similar organizations, in *Rationale*, I, 481–482, and II, 853–856, suggests that it is well rooted in the past. The Beggar's Benison, a men's club which flourished in Scotland in the eighteenth and nineteenth centuries, included as part of its ceremony the ritual exposure of the members' penises and masturbation into a silver dish called the "Test Platter," as well as, in a manner smacking of pre-adolescent voyeurism, the examination of the genitals of a girl, designated as a "heroine" of the society.

82. Clarence Had Hard Luck

Told by Walter J. Hazlewood, Eureka Springs, Ark., May, 1952. He had it from a lady at Hot Springs, Ark., in 1946.

One time there was a boy named Clarence, that drove the delivery wagon for Hogan's meat-market. He got to sparking a rich man's daughter named Louise, and she thought Clarence was wonderful. The rich man didn't like it much, but finally he let 'em get married. The next morning Louise was dead, and it looks like Clarence has fucked her to death in one night.

About six months after that Clarence got to sparking another girl, and her name was Maisie. She thought Clarence was wonderful, too. Maisie's folks hollered like hell, but him and her run off and got married anyhow. The next morning Maisie was dead, and it looks like Clarence has fucked her to death, just like he done Louise.

About six months after that Clarence got to sparking a girl named Betty, and he wants to get married right off. Betty thought about it awhile, and then she says, "Clarence, let's you and me go for a walk." They went out in the woods, and Betty laid down under a tree. "Come on, Clarence," she says, "let's see what you've got." Clarence jumped onto her, and done the best he could. But it wasn't much, because his pecker was only about two inches long.

Betty didn't say nothing at the time except that she decided not to marry Clarence. But about ten years later, after Clarence got killed a-fighting the policeman in Okmulgee, she told Gram French all about it. "My goodness," says Gram, "what do you reckon happened to Louise and Maisie?" Betty just laughed. "I believe them girls broke their backs," she says, "a-trying to get a little fucking out of Clarence!"

[X712.2.1.5]
This is related to a number of similar stories of the wife's complaint about the man with the small penis (see Numbers 45 and 75 of this collection). Legman, *Rationale,* I, 674–675, suggests that it belongs to that small group of jokes of character reversal, in which the man is put down for his sexual inadequacy.

83. Married by the Lord

Told by J. E. Dunwoody, Clinton, Iowa, March, 1951. He heard it in McDonald County, Mo., about 1910.

One time there was a country girl walked up and throwed her drawers into the wash kettle. "Sally," says her maw, "what do you mean, running around without no pants on?" Sally just giggled, and she says, "I don't need 'em, because I'm married now." The old woman looked at her. "How could you be married," says she, "when there ain't a preacher in fifty miles?"

Sally laughed some more, and scratched herself. "The Lord married me and Zeke this morning, right here in Dog Holler," she says. "The Lord provides, and them He joins together let no man put ass-under. Zeke says Nature is calling us right now, and let the Lord have His way. So we pulled off our clothes, and Zeke laid down on top of me. He stuck his jemson in my fork, and it sure did feel good. Zeke done a lot of pushing down, so I pushed up. We got to going mighty fast, and breathing hard. Then all of a sudden I went stone blind, but the Lord restored my sight. Blessed be His holy name!"

The old woman just stood there with her mouth open. "My God, Sally," she says, "you ain't married at all! You've went and fucked a silly chore-boy, that don't know enough to pour piss out of a boot!" But Sally just laughed louder than ever. "Don't you believe it, Maw," says she. "There ain't no spindle-assed preacher in the world could join anybody tighter than the Lord joined me and Zeke, right here in Dog Holler!"

It looks like Sally was right, at that. Her and Zeke just kept on a-doing it, and raised a fine big family. They got along about as good as any married folks, and you might say they lived happy ever after.

[X732.4.1]

I have not found anything to parallel this story. The claim to having been married by the Lord is, in effect, an extension of the concept of marriage and divorce practiced by the New Ground religion (see Number 75 of this collection, "The Little End of Nothing").

84. The Girls from Joplin

Told by an elderly gentleman in Neosho, Mo., February, 1928. He thought it was a true story, and said that such incidents were not uncommon in the 1890's.

One time there was an empty house up on Honey Creek, and two girls from Joplin moved in. Them young hussies would screw anybody for thirty-five cents, and if a man didn't have no money they'd take cornmeal or sidemeat. Some little boys stayed out of school to hang around there, and the girls would suck their peckers just for the hell of it. The womenfolks in the neighborhood warned 'em to move out, but the little bitches just laughed. Next night there was a bundle of sticks hanging on the gate, but they didn't pay no attention.

About a week after that a bunch of women drug 'em out, and here they come down the road in broad daylight. Them Joplin girls didn't have a stitch on, only their hands was tied together with carpet-rags. The womenfolks had cut switches, and they tanned 'em every step of the way. Some of the women kept a-pounding on tin pans, and the little sluts was hollering so loud you could hear 'em clear to the post office. Every house they went past, the people would run out to look, just like it was a circus. You never seen such fancy dancing. There ain't nothing livelier than two young whores with a hickory on their ass.

The womenfolks drummed 'em all the way to the county line, which it is pretty near three miles. Then somebody untied their hands, and give 'em two decent calico dresses. "If you-uns ever come back," says old lady Mosely, "it will be a regular blacksnake next time, instead of these little switches." But them girls just high-tailed it up the highway, and none of the home folks ever seen 'em again.

There is plenty of peckerwood gals around here that might do a little fucking sometimes, but they ain't brazen about it like the whores in them big towns. If the people in Joplin want to hang around cat-houses, that's their business. But we sure don't aim to have nothing like that on Honey Creek.

[Q243.1.3]

This is unquestionably a local anecdote, but the situation, in which the small community takes the law into its own hands in eliminating prostitution, undoubtedly has been repeated many times. Randolph gives several references: his own *The Ozarks*, pp. 54–55; Williamson, *The Woods Colt*, pp. 142–163; and George Milburn, *Julie*, pp. 185–188.

85. Bit by a Spider

Told by Frank Pickett, Eureka Springs, Ark., December, 1951. He said it was a true account of something that happened near Joplin, Mo., in the early 1900's.

One time there was a fellow named Higley that run around a little sometimes, and finally he got a dose of the old bullhead clap. So his wife noticed that he never screwed her for several days, and she got to wondering. Higley was scared to tell the old woman what was the matter, and he sure didn't want to give her the clap. But something has got to be done, because he knowed she wasn't going to be put off much longer.

It was just about daybreak when Higley got a grand idea. All of a sudden he give a loud yell, and jumped clear out of the bed. "Great God!" says he, "I'm bit by a goddam spider!" And then he cussed his wife for not keeping the house clean, and he says things has come to a pretty pass when spiders is crawling right into a man's bed, and maybe it is one of them poison tarantulers for all I know! Old lady Higley could see his prick was red and swelled up, so she sent for the doctor.

Doc Holton seen right away how things was, but he never cracked a smile. "It's a spider, all right," says he, "and a mighty bad case at that. You come to my office every day for treatment. Whatever you do, don't sleep with your wife till that spider-bite is plumb cured up." So then Doc walked out, and Higley went and laid down in the spare bedroom.

Well sir, old Higley went down to Doc's office pretty regular for awhile, and he grumbled a lot about how lonesome it is in the spare bedroom all by himself. But everything worked out all right in the end, and Higley's wife never did suspicion what was the matter, the time he got the old bull-head clap.

[K 1876]
This belongs to the category of Deceptions by Disguise or Illusion; Thompson, *Motif-Index* (K1800–K1899). Although there are no close parallels, Thompson notes a number of related items, including the stabbing of a bag of blood to give the illusion of wounding (K1875).

86. The Duck-Hunter's Woman

Told by Ern Long, Joplin, Mo., August, 1931, as a true story.
He credited it to a guide on the Cowskin River, near Noel,
Mo.

One time there was some rich people come down from
Kansas City. The men would go duck-hunting up the river
every day, while their womenfolks stayed at the clubhouse by
the old mill. Mostly they didn't look like much, but there
was one terrible pretty woman in the bunch, and all the men
for miles around was trying to get next to her. But she just
turned up her nose, and wouldn't pay them no mind.

There was a big farmer boy named Elbert come to town,
but he couldn't get no job in the clubhouse. The only thing
Elbert could do was whittle those decoy ducks out of cedar
wood, and then paint 'em up for the hunters. The pretty
woman come by where Elbert was a-whittling, and she noticed how his pants was sticking out. That same night she
brushed up against Elbert a-standing on the steps, while the
rich people was having a big party in the dining room.

Next morning the pretty woman told Elbert stop at her
room, the first chance he got. She didn't have enough clothes
on to wad a shotgun, so Elbert give her a good screwing.
After that they just laid there awhile, and she kept a-feeling
of his tallywhacker. "This is a nice little pecker, boy," she
says, "but what become of that monstrous big one you had
yesterday?" Elbert picked up his overalls where they was laying on the floor, and pulled out a club about fourteen inches
long. "That's my decoy," says he. "I made it out of cedar
wood, same as I do the ducks."

Well sir, she set up for a minute, a-staring at that thing in
Elbert's hand. Then the pretty woman just fell back in the
bed, and laughed till the tears rolled down her cheeks. Her

and Elbert tore off one more chunk, and then he went back to the carpenter shop.

The rich people all went home next day, but the pretty woman bought one of them wooden ducks just before they left. It will make a nice keepsake, she says, because you don't see no decoys like Elbert's in Kansas City.

[K1329]

Lockridge, *Waggish Tales*, pp. 131–144, gives a lengthy, involved tale, with the last episode building up to the deception of the "decoy." Hall, *Anecdota*, I, No. 248, follows the form of Randolph's version, except that it is presented in Negro dialect. A brief, updated version appears as No. 350 in the same collection; a girl comments on the profile of a famous actor. Her companion says that if she means halfway down, those are just keys. *Anecdota*, II, No. 329, is another brief variant, once more in Negro dialect, in which the girl asks her boyfriend if he loves her or does he just have a jackknife in his pocket.

87. Travelers Are All Fools

Told by Elbert Short, Crane, Mo., June, 1933. It is an old story, he says, that was popular near Marionville, Mo., in the 1920's.

One time there was a pretty widow-woman that lived all by herself. Lots of the country boys wanted to lay up with her, but she says a farmer ain't no good, because he can't do nothing but shovel shit and holler "Gee!" There's plenty of women like her, and they think travelers is smarter than us fellows that was raised right here in the country.

Well, a stranger stopped at her place the night of the big storm, and he couldn't go no further because the river was up. "I'm all alone here," says the widow-woman, "and I only got one bed. But you can stay all night, if you behave like a gentleman." So the fellow slept on his side of the bed, and he never even touched her. The widow-woman was pretty disgusted, but she didn't say nothing.

It wasn't long till the river got up again, and there was another traveler wanted to stay all night, so she let him in. "Well," says he, "do you want me to treat you like my wife, or like a stranger?" The widow-woman thought awhile, and then she says "Treat me like your wife." The man says "All right, lady. It's your house." So then the fellow turned his back on her, let a couple of big farts, and went to sleep. The widow-woman just laid there and gritted her teeth, but she never said nothing.

The widow-woman never let no travelers in after that, no matter if the river is up or not. She says traveling men are all fools nowadays, and it's better for respectable people not to have no truck with 'em.

[X724.3.1]
Ernest Baughman reported to Randolph that he heard this story in Indiana in 1945, and in New Mexico in 1954 and 1955. Legman, *Rationale*, I, 681–683, discusses the story and its variants at some length, identifying its core as an expression of sexual hatred. He also provides two interesting variants. In one, from New York in 1945, a man and woman who are strangers to each other agree to share a room in a crowded hotel if a partition is placed between the beds. She repeatedly awakens him with the request that he close the window a little. He finally asks if she'd like to be Mrs. Smith for the night, and when she eagerly replies in the affirmative, he tells her to get up and close the goddam window herself. In the other, from Orangeburg, N.Y., in 1944, the sex roles are reversed. A traveling saleswoman is put up with the farmer's son. She several times asks him to roll over to the other side of the bed, but he always gets up and runs around the

bed instead. When she says she doesn't think he knows what she wants, he replies that he certainly does, that she wants the whole damn bed but isn't going to get it.

88. The Baby Lost Weight

Told by George Head, Eureka Springs, Ark., July, 1948.

One time there was a young woman fetched a baby into Doc Henderson's office, and she says it is losing weight. Doc examined the baby awhile, and asked the woman about her victuals, but she says, "What I eat ain't got nothing to do with the baby being skinny." Doc figured she must be kind of stupid, so he didn't ask no more questions.

Doc examined her mighty careful, anyhow. And he pulled her dress open, to see if something is the matter with her breasts. The woman wiggled a good deal, but he sucked her tits, first one and then the other. There wasn't no milk at all. Finally she says, "That's my sister's baby, you know."

Old Doc Henderson was considerable set back when he heard that, because he never thought but what it was her baby. "Hell's fire," he says, "you shouldn't have come!" The young woman just kind of giggled. "I didn't," she says, "till you started a-sucking the second one."

[X711.2.1; X735.6.1]
Randolph notes a related item in Elgart, *Over Sexteen*, p. 146. The story hinges on the surprise or reversal of situation at the end; in the most widely known form of the story, it represents a much stronger put down of the doctor. A girl visits the doctor's office and is immediately told to disrobe for an examination. The doctor handles various parts of her body, asking each time if she knows what he is doing. He finally mounts her, and when he again poses his question, she answers that he's getting venereal

disease, which is what she came to him about. Buehler, in his master's thesis, pp. 12, 86, and 146, gives three versions, one from New York and two from Indiana. Legman, in his Introduction to *Rationale*, I, 36–37, traces the original form of the story to the *Oeuvres badines* of the eighteenth-century French poet Alexis Piron. A nobleman seduces a girl before reading her petition to him; afterward, he finds that it is a complaint against a doctor who failed to cure her of venereal disease. Legman further discusses the theme in *Rationale*, II, 367–368, and relates a version very similar to Randolph's heard in London in 1954.

The 1971 X-rated motion picture, "The Nurses," presents the same theme with reversed sex roles. A nurse, told to give a male patient a shot, finds him attractive and performs fellatio on him. Afterwards, she asks him what he's being treated for, and he tells her gonorrhea.

89. How Many Peters?

Told by William Hatton, Columbia, Mo., July, 1929. He heard it in Lawrence County, Mo., about 1905.

One time there was a buckbrush circuit-rider a-preaching about the time Jesus Christ got caught by the soldiers. It says in the Book that Peter cursed when the rooster crowed, and he denied Christ three times. The preacher wanted to show how lots of people is still denying Christ every day of their life, so all of a sudden he hollered out: "How many Peters is in this room?"

The church folks was plumb flabbergasted, and they just set there a-looking at each other. Of course the preacher didn't really mean pricks, but that's what it sounded like he meant. Pretty soon there was some young girls busted out laughing, and they couldn't stop. And then some boys took it up, so finally the marshal had to arrest 'em, and he marched the whole bunch down to the calaboose. The preacher kept a-gabbling about how they must be punished for interfering with Christian worship.

There was a infidel lawyer got up and says he will defend these children without no fee, because they never done nothing except giggle. "But that foul-mouthed preacher ought to be locked up," says he, "for telling the people to count peckers in the church house." The preacher raised a terrible holler when he heard that, but the church people didn't know what to think. There was a lot of talk about it, and finally old Squire Markham says to the marshal, "For God's sake turn them boys and girls loose, and let's forget the whole business."

The marshal turned the children loose, all right, but that lawyer and his friends was cracking jokes all over town. Everybody knows it is bad luck to poke fun at the Holy Scripture, but even some of the church folks had to laugh at them jokes. That poor preacher never showed up around here no more, and it's a good thing he didn't. A man like that ain't got no business a-preaching the gospel, anyhow.

[X455]
Randolph states that a related story was long remembered in Pineville, Mo. (see *Dialect Notes,* VI (1928), p. 61; Randolph, *The Ozarks,* p. 83). He also points out that some boys and girls were arrested and fined for giggling in a church at Caledonia, Mo. (Kansas City *Times,* August 15, 1935), and this action was endorsed editorially by several Missouri newspapers (Springfield *Leader and Press,* August 24, 1935). See also Randolph and Wilson, *Down in the Holler,* p. 101, quoted by Edward Sagarin, *The Anatomy of Dirty Words,* p. 74.

Buehler, in his master's thesis, pp. 23, 70, gives two variant forms. In one, from a Brooklyn informant, the priest announces that there will be a peter pulling contest at Saint Taffy's Cathedral. In the other, from a native of Indiana, the preacher, thoroughly flustered by a girl who is playing up to him in church, tells her that she must change her ways or when she comes to those Pearly Gates, Saint Finger will point his peter at her. The name "Peter" has an irresistible attraction for punsters.

90. The Hollyhock Story

Told by Pete Woolsey, Pineville, Mo., September, 1924.

One time there was a fellow that come down a new-cut road, and he got to diddling a waitress at the tavern. They would go for a walk after she got off work, and just lay down under a bush or up against a haystack somewheres. Several times they done it right in town, behind one of these here billboards. He was a stout young fellow, and the waitress thought he was God's own cousin.

Finally a big rain come up before they could get home, so he took her to a tourist cabin. It was the first time they ever got together in a regular bed. There was a electric light too, and they read awhile in a seed catalogue that was in the cabin, because there wasn't no magazines handy. Then he put the blocks to her again, and both of them went to sleep.

When the waitress woke up about five o'clock, her boyfriend was gone. After awhile she found a note on the table. But when she went to read it, he had just wrote one word, *Hollyhock.* The girl couldn't make out what he meant, till she seen the seed catalogue a-laying there. She fingered through the pages to *Hollyhock,* and there was one line marked with a pencil. "Fine behind privies and barns," it said, "but not much good in beds."

Everybody kept a sharp lookout for the fellow after that,

because the waitress says she is going to give him a piece of her mind. But he never showed up at the tavern no more, and it looks like he must have went to some other town.

[X735.10.1]
Randolph remarks that he heard this related at Aurora, Mo., in 1951 as a "brand new joke." Ernest Baughman informed Randolph that he heard it in Albuquerque in 1954. Robert Adams heard it in Martinsville, Ind., in 1963, while collecting jokes on rural characters and situations for his master's thesis. Legman, *Rationale*, I, 675, gives a version heard in Minnesota in 1946, in which a man calls his new bride "Hollyhock."

91. He Couldn't Stand Nastiness

Told by Otho Pratt, Verona, Mo., July, 1951. He heard it near Horse Creek, in Stone County, Mo., about 1935.

One time there was a young farmer had some folks come over to his place for supper. The fellow's wife didn't know how to cook much, and the house looked kind of dirty, but everybody was eating the best they could. The people that live on Horse Creek are all hell for politeness, because they don't want to hurt nobody's feelings.

Just then the baby come a-crawling out on the floor, and you could see where he has shit all over himself. The kid's mother didn't pay no attention, but the man spoke right up. "Marthy," says he, "fetch the dishrag, and wipe that young-un's ass. If there's one thing I can't stand, it's nastiness!"

The folks that was eating just gulped, and took another gander at them dishes. It wasn't no place for anybody that has got a weak stomach. Even the boys that ain't too particular begun to feel kind of uneasy. They didn't go there for supper no more, and pretty soon the fellow give up farming and moved into town. It was a long time ago, but the folks never did forget him. That crack he made about nastiness is kind of a joke on Horse Creek, to this day.

[X716.4.1]
This is related to Number 36 of this collection, "That Boy Needs Pants," in that both situations are played off against dinner guests, who are faced with finishing a meal after witnessing their hosts' actions and remarks. Another related story comes from Belgium; *Kryptadia*, IV, 314–315. In that one the priest notices that his servant doesn't bother to wipe herself after relieving herself at the roadside, and he remarks that that is why his balls are always so full of shit.

92. The City Girl and the Cow

Told by J. L. Russell, Harrison, Ark., April, 1950. It was regarded as a new story by the boys around Alpena, Ark., in 1907.

One time there was a girl named Nellie come to our neighborhood, but she was born and raised in a big city. Nellie hadn't never seen a farm before, and she couldn't tell a bull from a cow. But people from them big towns always let on like they know everything, so Nellie didn't ask no questions.

It looked funny to her when the boys fetched in the milk, because Nellie thought milk come in bottles on the front porch. The womenfolks told how they milked the critters, but Nellie figured maybe they was kidding her. After while she took a little bucket and went out to the barn by herself. There was only one cow in sight, and Nellie sure was surprised when she seen them big tits. "My God," she says, "he's got four of 'em!" When she come back to the house, her bucket was still empty. "There's something wrong with that animal," says Nellie. "I done everything I know, but them spigots just stayed limber!"

The womenfolks pretty near died laughing when they heard that, and some of 'em kept a-giggling for a long time. Nellie didn't go to the barn no more, but she never did understand what them country women was laughing about.

[J1731.3]
Rural humor abounds with stories of the city person who is ignorant of farm life. Thompson, *Motif-Index*, assigns this a subheading under J1731, with examples from Estonia and Spain. Much of this humor in the United States deals with identification of the sex of farm animals, particularly cattle. Legman, *Rationale*, I, 225, notes a variant collected in Minnesota in 1935, in which the city girl says she milked the cows and everything, and the farm hand observed that that must have been a surprise to the bulls. In another variant (p. 137) heard in New York in 1939, the schoolmarm's heifer is to be serviced, and she takes it to the bull. The owner of the bull hears a commotion and rushes out to learn the trouble. The schoolmarm complains that they can't make the heifer lie down.

93. Ambrose Done All Right

Told by Clyde Harris, Tar River, Okla., July, 1927. He heard it near Huntsville, Ark., in 1910.

One time some people was having a dance up on Plow Handle Mountain, and a big half-wit boy named Ambrose come around. He was looking for a piece of cock, but the girls didn't want no part of Ambrose. When he asked Sue Merton to go out in the brush with him, she just kicked up her heels and laughed right in his face.

Ambrose kept a-pestering every woman that come along, and finally they made it up to play a joke on him. A big girl named Lulu wrapped some fresh cow-shit in a piece of gunnysack, and led Ambrose out behind the barn. She laid down with the gunnysack betwixt her legs, and when he climbed on she guided his pecker right into the cow-shit. Ambrose begun to bounce up and down something wonderful, but pretty soon Lulu says "Honey, I don't believe you've got it in very good." So then she reached her hand down to fix things.

"No! No! Don't you do it!" says Ambrose, and he begun to grunt louder than ever. "If you got anything better than this, I don't want it!" says he. The other girls was peeking around the corner, and they all busted out laughing. But the big half-wit has got his gun off by this time, and he didn't care if anybody seen him or not. He just walked right out before all them people, a-wiping the cow-shit off'n his tool with a big red hankerchief. The home folks pretty near died laughing, and some of 'em talked like the joke wasn't on Ambrose at all. Lulu got pretty mad, and so did her boy-friend. There was hard words spoke, and some blood spilled, before that dance broke up at daylight.

[J1251.4]
Randolph states that he has several versions of this story, and that J. C. Edwards, Webster Groves, Mo., says it was a man disguised in petticoats who held the cow dung between his legs. Legman, *Rationale*, I, 538, 679, gives two additional versions. One, heard on a transcontinental train in 1943, has the man mounting the girl under some bushes in the park. First he's in the dirt, then in the right place, and finally he decides to go back into the dirt. The other, heard in New York in 1963, is the same,

with the substitution of a sandy beach for the park. He notes that
it also appears in *Sex to Sexty*, VI, No. 21.

94. The Prick Teaser

*Told by J. L. Russell, Harrison, Ark., April, 1950. He heard
it near Green Forest, Ark., in the late 1880's.*

One time there was a country boy seen a girl at the town
dance, that acted hotter than a two-dollar pistol. They went
out in the brush, but she says there ain't going to be no
fucking, because she promised her Pappy not to. The country boy felt of her legs, and patted her bottom, and kissed
her bubbies, and then he begun to tickle her twitchet. The
girl says things like that is just natural, and her Pappy never
told her not to do it.

Pretty soon they was both stark naked, a-romping around
on the grass like a couple of minks. She says there ain't no
harm for a nice girl to take off her clothes and play with a
gentleman's tallywhacker, because Pappy never told her not
to. The girl kept a-tickling his balls with her finger, and she
licked his pecker with her tongue, too. The country boy just
about went crazy, but he couldn't get it in her, because she
promised Pappy not to do no fucking.

About that time the country boy got to breathing awful
fast, and then he just laid still for awhile. "Your Pappy is a
mighty smart fellow," says he, "and what does a man like that
foller for a living?" She answered that her Pappy is the best
paper-hanger in town. "Well, here's some paste for him,"
says the country boy, and he smeared a handful of duckbutter
right under the town girl's nose. So then the country boy put
on his clothes and went back to the dance. He ought to have

give her a kick in the ass for good measure, but the story don't say nothing about that.

[X723.1.1]

This is related to Aarne-Thompson Type 853A, "No," in which the clever man gains his desires by skillfully framing his questions, so that the girl's "No" becomes in fact a "Yes." This form appears in Afanasiev, *Stories*, pp. 42–45, and is known widely in folksong form as "Oh, No, John," "The Spanish Merchant's Daughter," and various other titles. In Randolph's tale there is one "No," the ultimate one, and it is not violated. Accordingly, instead of gaining the girl, the boy rejects her. Hall, *Anecdota*, II, No. 341, is a very condensed form of the same story, in which the joke element is almost completely lost. There is a related tale which is from Belgium; *Kryptadia*, IV, 341–342. The husband attempts amorous play while his wife is saying her prayers, and she stops him. Later, when she begins amorous play, he sarcastically asks if she takes his balls to be the beads of her rosary.

95. Lincoln Took a Drink

Told by Otho Pratt, Verona, Mo., July, 1951. He heard it near Horse Creek, in Stone County, Mo., about 1914.

One time there was an old man lived at the mouth of Horse Creek, and he used to tell a story about Abe Lincoln. The old fellow claims he seen it in the Saint Louis *Post-Dispatch*, but that must be a lie because everybody knowed he didn't have no book-learning, so how could he read anything out of a newspaper? And also they got a law against things like that, and a dirty story couldn't be printed in the paper anyhow.

But the way old Horse Creek told it, Abe Lincoln went into a saloon. "What will you have this morning?" says the bartender. Abe Lincoln ordered up an egg-poop, and the man mixed it for him. Just then a country fellow sidled up to the bar, and the bartender asked what he wanted. "I'll take the same as Mister Lincoln," says the country boy.

The saloon keeper stirred up something in a glass and set it on the bar. The country fellow took a swig, and then he made a terrible bad face. "Mister Lincoln," says he, "maybe that bartender just pooped in your drink. But he sure as hell shit in mine!" And with that the country boy walked right out of the saloon.

The old man that lived on Horse Creek says Abe Lincoln told the story himself, and that's why they put it in the Saint Louis *Post-Dispatch*. But it don't seem likely the President would go around telling tales like that, while there is a big war going on. So the folks figured that the old man just made it up out of his own head, and President Lincoln never even heard of such a thing.

[X716.5]
Abraham Lincoln's humble origins and his unaffected manner have made him the subject of an entire cycle of jokes and stories, many of them quite earthy. Another example from the cycle may be found in Hall, *Anecdota*, I, No. 340, in which Lincoln is introduced to the Bates family, concluding with young Master Bates. Turning to the father, Lincoln says, "Make him stop. It's a bad habit." *Anecdota*, II, No. 16 is a variant of Randolph's story without Lincoln. A country boy trying to appear sophisticated steps up to a bar and asks for a "billiard." The bartender winks to the other customers, goes to the back room, and urinates in a glass. The boy blows off the foam, drinks it down, and then remarks that if he hadn't been drinking billiards for years he'd have sworn that was piss.

96. The Circus Come to Town

Told by Elbert Short, Crane, Mo., June, 1933. The story is widely known.

One time there was a circus come to this town with elephants, and some of the folks got excited, because their horses broke loose, and also the people here hadn't never seen nothing like that before. Old man Massey thought the elephants must be a fake with leather on the outside, and never did believe it till he seen one of 'em shit right in front of the courthouse. Most of us knowed better, of course. But twenty years after the circus had come and went, the fellows around town was still cracking jokes about them elephants.

The boys used to tell how one of 'em got loose when the red wagons pulled into East Elsey. Next morning old Biddy Walters come to the sheriff's office. She says there is a tremendous big animal in her turnip patch, and it will have to be got rid of. The sheriff knowed what it was, but he asked the old woman a lot of questions just for fun, because there was some town folks a-listening. "What is the critter doing in your garden patch?" he says. "The goddam thing is a-walking backwards," says Biddy Walters, "pulling up turnips with his tail!"

The town folks laughed when they heard that, and Biddy begun to get mad. The sheriff just shook his head, and he says maybe Mistress Walters better go somewheres and lay down, because the hot sun don't agree with her. The old woman was so goddam mad she couldn't talk for a minute, so the sheriff says, "What else is the monster a-doing?" Biddy Walters just scowled at him. "You won't believe it," she says, "but I'm going to tell you, anyhow. The last I seen of the varmint, he was a-sticking my turnips up his ass!"

It don't look like anybody would be so ignorant as that, in this day and generation. But the folks that knowed Biddy

Walters still tell the tale, and every one of 'em swears it is the God's truth.

[J1903.4.1]
Ernest Baughman reported to Randolph that he had heard the story in Albuquerque in 1948, with the woman answering the officer's last question with, "Officer, if I told you, you'd never believe me!" Further versions of the story may be found in Lockridge, *Waggish Tales*, pp. 51–53, and Hall, *Anecdota*, II, No. 418. Legman, *Rationale*, I, 137, states that the story has been printed in many collections, most recently in Elgart, *Over Sexteen*, p. 44. In *Rationale*, II, 826, he relates a version taken from *The Cotton Ginner's Journal*, October, 1938. It is similar to Baughman's, but with a small boy instead of a woman reporting to the police.

97. It Was a Good Answer

Told by Joe Ingenthron, Forsyth, Mo., June, 1940. He heard it near Walnut Shade, Mo., about 1916.

One time there was a country boy that run after Mary Lou Bixby, but him and her fell out about something, because she was very jealous. So then the country boy went to one of them big towns, and maybe he took a few drinks. A pretty girl was just going to the dance hall, so he followed her in, and it wasn't long till they was dancing the worst you ever seen. The lights was kind of dim, and the pretty girl run her hand down in the country boy's pants. There wasn't no money in the pockets, but she got hold of his pecker anyhow. It looked like he was going to screw her right then and there, but all of a sudden them town people got to fighting. Pretty soon they begun to fire off pistols, and things went on like that till the policemen busted up the dance. The worst of it was that a stray bullet hit the country boy in the nuts, so he was laid up at the town hospital for three weeks.

Soon as the doctors got him cured the country boy come back home, and he says, "No more of them big towns for me." Next day him and Mary Lou Bixby was walking home from Sunday School and he told her what happened, only he didn't say nothing about the pretty girl in the dance hall. They set down under a tree, but soon as Mary Lou Bixby seen them scars she kind of pushed him away. "It looks to me like you was shot from in front," she says. So the country boy says yes, that's right. "Well," says Mary Lou, "how come the bullet didn't hit your tallywhacker?"

That was a pretty hard question, but the country boy just grinned. "I was thinking about you when the shooting started," says he, "so naturally it was a-standing straight up, just like it is right now!" Anybody could see that his pecker was sticking up out of harm's way. So then Mary Lou Bixby had to laugh, and rolled over on her back. Maybe she didn't believe everything he said, but it was a mighty good answer anyhow. Him and her got along pretty good from then on, and I reckon they lived happy ever after.

[X712.3.1.1]
Legman, *Rationale,* II, 445, offers several forms of this story, heard in New York in 1939, Berkeley in 1943, and Washington, D.C., in 1952. In all of these versions a soldier has suffered the wound on the battlefield, and his reply when asked about the wound in the hospital takes two forms. In one, the answer is similar to Randolph's—the man was thinking about a girl. In the other, a woman's inquiry about where the soldier was wounded brings the response, "If it had been you, the bullet would have missed." Other tales about injury to the testicles may be found in Lockridge, *Waggish Tales,* pp. 192–193, and *Kryptadia,* IV, 305–307 (from Belgium).

98. He Changed Her Tire

Told by Lon Jordan, Farmington, Ark., January, 1942.

One time there was a girl come driving along in a fine automobile, and all of a sudden one of the tires went flat. There wasn't nobody in sight, so she jacked up the wheel and tried to change it herself. But the wrench kept a-slipping, and the taps was too tight. She pulled and done her damndest, but it wasn't no use.

Just then a big old farm boy come along, and she says do you know how to change a tire? The farm boy says yes, so the girl set down and rested while he put on her spare. When the job was done, she says, "How much do I owe you?" The big farm boy looked her over. "Folks around here just kind of swap, mostly," says he.

The town girl thought she knowed what he meant, and they walked over behind some wind-blowed trees. "You can have anything I got," she says, and pulled the dress up over her head. Then she took her pants off, and hung 'em on a bush. The big farm boy felt of the dress careful, and he says, "It ain't wool." He run his fingers over the pink silk panties. "Them flimsy things ain't no good," says he. The girl just stood there with her mouth a-hanging open. "Give me twenty-five cents," says the big farm boy, "and we'll call it square." She handed him a quarter, so then the big farm boy walked on down the road.

After he was gone the girl put her clothes on, and pretty soon she drive back to town. Her folks wanted to know what is the matter. "I never been so insulted in my whole life," she says. The folks kept asking all kinds of questions, but the girl says it is none of their business, and she never did tell 'em what happened.

Ernest Baughman informed Randolph that he had heard the story in Indiana in 1935, with a bicycle instead of a car, and the boy took the bicycle. Legman, *Rationale*, I, 93, reports Baughman's form of the story, from Norfolk, Va., in 1953. He also notes a homosexual variant, from New York in 1953, in which a movie star takes off her clothes and offers the homosexual anything he wants. He takes her car.

99. Rosie Got Even

Told by Martin Travis, Joplin, Mo., December, 1926. It is a very old story; I heard it in Pittsburg, Kans., as long ago as 1907.

One time there was a fellow from Joplin that was going with a pretty little girl named Rosie. She give him her maidenhead all right, after he promised they would get married next week, but all of a sudden the son-of-a-bitch run off. Rosie didn't believe nothing any man said after that, and the folks kicked her out. She got kind of tough then, and just lived around in the hotel where she could screw the traveling salesmen.

It was several years later when the porter sent a man up to Rosie's room, and it was the same fellow that got her maidenhead. Rosie let him in just like anybody else, but soon as he seen who it was the son-of-a-bitch begun to give her hell. "It looks like you could be true to somebody, and live decent," says he. "But here you are, a-fucking these traveling men for money!" She tried to talk nice to him, but he just kept on a-hollering about how she is nothing but a whore now, and he don't want nothing to do with her.

Pretty soon Rosie says, "Well, it ain't no use crying about what's past and gone. I was a good girl once, so let's have a drink for old time's sake." But the fellow says, "Hell no, I wouldn't touch none of your whiskey, because you want to get me drunk and steal my wallet." Rosie just looked at him a minute, and walked over to a pitcher with some roses in it. "Take this here flower," says she, "because it is fresh and pretty, like I used to be. But pretty soon the petals will fall off, and the leaves dry up. There won't be nothing left but a crooked stem with thorns on it, like I am now." The son-of-a-bitch just stood there with the rose in his hand.

"When that time comes," says Rosie, "I want you to think of me. And then you can take the dry stem with the thorns on it, and stick it up your ass!" She pushed the bell with her foot, and in come two big porters that was Rosie's friends. "This pimp wants me to leave you boys," she says, "and work in a house at Kansas City." So then the porters beat the living shit out of him, and took his money. He begun to holler for the law, but the deputy sheriff was a friend of Rosie, too. The deputy give the fellow another good beating, and run him plumb out of town. It served the son-of-a-bitch right, and that is the end of the story.

[Q243.2.0.1]
Lockridge, *Waggish Tales,* pp. 201–216, gives an extended version of the tale, in which the boy is not directly responsible for the girl's downfall and does not receive a beating. However, he is saddled with a moral guilt through his acceptance of a double standard of morality, and the story again concludes with the symbol of the rose.

100. The Folks on Rumpus Ridge

Told by Frank Payne, Galena, Mo., November, 1932. He says it was a common story in Stone County, Mo., about 1906.

One time there was an old couple that lived on Rumpus Ridge, and they had a terrible pretty daughter. It was just about dark when a stranger come along, and he says, "I have got lost, and will you let me stay all night?" They give him the spare room, and he watched careful to see where the pretty girl's bed was. After everybody had went to sleep, the town fellow sneaked over there. But the girl and her mother had traded places, so she got screwed by mistake. The old woman giggled, and the stranger was pretty mad, but there wasn't nothing he could do about it.

Pretty soon somebody come walking past in their bare feet, and the town fellow knowed the pretty girl had went back to her own bed. After awhile he slipped over there again, and crawled in with the pretty girl. She was glad of it, and you never seen such a shagging match. The stranger stayed there a long time, and it was pretty near daylight when he got back to the spare room.

Next morning the old man just set in the kitchen, with a shotgun right by his chair. There wasn't much said, but the town fellow felt kind of uneasy. He eat some breakfast though, and got ready to leave. "How much do I owe you?" says he. The old farmer just looked at him. "I don't charge nobody for bed and victuals," says he, "but this here breaking up people's family is a bad business." The town fellow was shaking like holly in a high wind. "I don't care about the old woman," says the farmer, "because she's limbered enough pricks to build a bridge over James River. But Lucy is just a innocent child, and never screwed nobody but me in her whole life." With that the old man picked up the shotgun, and he cocked both hammers.

The town fellow stood there with his mouth open, and he didn't know whether to shit or go blind. But finally he says, "Well, I am always willing to do the right thing." The old farmer studied awhile, and then he let one hammer of the shotgun down easy. "Stranger," says he, "do you think three dollars is too much?" The town fellow give him the money, and then the old man let the other hammer down easy.

The pretty girl was hanging some clothes out behind the house, and she waved at the town fellow when he walked on down the road. But the town fellow never looked back. "I don't care about the money," says he, "it's the principle of the thing." And nobody likes to be scared out of a year's growth with a shotgun, neither.

[K1317.5.1; X724.5.1; X724.6.1]
Randolph cites related yarns in Wilson, *Backwoods America*, pp. 37–39, and Lockridge, *Waggish Tales*, pp. 117–122. Lockridge also gives another related story (pp. 106–109) in which the traveler enters the wrong room and unwittingly seduces the girl's aged grandmother, who thereupon dies with a beautiful smile on her face.

101. She Named the Town

Told by Johnny Shrader, Eureka Springs, Ark., July, 1954. Shrader is an old lead-miner from Jasper County, Mo., and he heard the story near Joplin in the early 1900's.

One time there was a bunch of Pukes lived over by Joplin, at a camp knowed as Minersville. The boys didn't have nothing but picks and shovels in them days, and maybe a windlass with a bucket. They just gophered around in prospect holes, because there wasn't no powder to speak of. Whenever they hit hard rock they would quit, and dig a new hole some-wheres else. What they dug up was mostly white-looking ore that they called dry-bone or turkey-fat. There was lead in the stuff, though, and you could trade it for groceries at the store.

Old lady Bradley was running the boarding-house at Min-ersville then, and she had a pretty girl named Myrtle to wait on the table. Them overall boys was always a-following Myrtle around, but she never done no screwing unless they paid her first. A fellow named Taylor come down with the horn colic one night, but he didn't have the two dollars. Taylor kept hollering how he'd have the money come Saturday night, but Myrtle just laughed, because she'd heard that song before. "Fetch me a gunnysack full of turkey-fat," she says, "and we'll talk business." Taylor begun to cry like a baby, but he didn't have no turkey-fat neither. "Bawling won't buy nothing at the store," says Myrtle. "It's ore, or no go!"

The walls in that boarding-house was just thin slabs, with-out no plaster. Everybody in the house could hear what Myrtle told Taylor, and them prospectors just laughed their-self sick. It was kind of a joke in all the saloons, and finally they held a meeting to change the name of the camp. Miners-ville don't sound very good anyhow, but *ore-or-no-go* is kind of high toned. It all happened pretty near eighty years ago, but the name stuck. You can see Oronogo painted right on the post office window, any time you feel like driving up Main Street.

[A1617.1]

Randolph provides excellent documentation for the naming of Oronogo, Mo. The town of Oronogo really was called Miners-ville in the early days (Dolph Shaner, *The Story of Joplin,* p. 4), but nobody knows just how the present name came to be adopted. Stevens, *The Ozark Uplift,* p. 10, says that a miner called his partner to come out of the shaft to attend a circus.

"Ore, or no go," was the answer, and thus the camp got its name. Ramsay, *Our Storehouse of Missouri Place Names,* p. 116, repeats a local legend about somebody who said, "It's *ore or no go!*" Ramsay adds, however, that such yarns are "too good to be true," and that Oronogo is probably a distorted Spanish name. A very similar Oronogo story is found in Hedgecock, *Gone Are the Days,* p. 10.

Legman, *Rationale,* II, 322, offers a related bawdy version of how Yuma, Ariz., received its name. I might add that despite the relatively short time span of American history, particularly of its interior regions, the origins of countless place names can be accounted for only through oral tradition. There are literally scores of books and articles which record place name legends.

Bibliography

Aarne, Antti, and Stith Thompson. *The Types of the Folktale.* Helsinki, 1961.

Abrahams, Roger. *Deep Down in the Jungle.* Hatboro, Pa., 1964; Chicago, 1970.

Afanasiev, Aleksandr. *Stories from the Folklore of Russia.* Paris, 1897.

Allsopp, Fred W. *Folklore of Romantic Arkansas.* 2 vols. New York, 1931.

Baughman, Ernest. *Type and Motif-Index of the Folktales of England and North America.* Bloomington, Ind., 1966.

Brewer, J. Mason. *The Word on the Brazos.* Austin, Texas, 1953.

Buehler, Richard. "An Annotated Collection of Contemporary Obscene Humor from the Bloomington Campus of Indiana University." M.A. thesis, Indiana University, 1964.

Cerf, Bennett. *Anything for a Laugh.* New York, 1946.

Chase, Richard. *American Folk Tales and Songs.* New York, 1956.

Clugston, W. G. *Facts You Should Know about Arkansas.* Girard, Kans., 1928.

Cunningham, Robert Hays. *Amusing Prose Chap-Books.* London and Glasgow, 1889.

Curran, William. *Clean Dirt.* Williamsport, Pa., 1938.

Dacus, J. A., and James W. Buel. *A Tour of St. Louis, or the Inside Life of a Great City.* St. Louis, 1878.

Day, Donald, ed. *Publications of the Texas Folklore Society,* XIX. Austin, Texas, 1944.

Duncan, Bob. *The Dickey Bird Was Singing.* New York, 1952.

Elgart, J. M. *Over Sexteen.* New York, 1951.

———. *Still More Over Sexteen.* New York, 1954.

Gould, George, and Walter Pyle. *Anomalies and Curiosities of Medicine*. New York, 1896.

Hall, J. Mortimer [Joseph Fliesler]. *Anecdota Americana*. Boston [New York?], 1927.

———. *Anecdota Americana*, second series. Boston [New York?], 1934.

Hedgecock, L. J. *Gone Are the Days*. Girard, Kans., 1949.

Hoosier Folklore Bulletin. Bloomington, Ind., 1942–45.

Journal of American Folklore. 1888–

Kryptadia. 12 vols. Heilbronn and Paris, 1883–1911.

[Landesman, Jay, and Gershon Legman, eds.] *Neurotica*. Nos. 1–9, 1948–51.

[Legman, G.] *The Limerick*. Paris, 1953.

Legman, G. *Rationale of the Dirty Joke, First Series*. New York, 1968.

———. *No Laughing Matter: Rationale of the Dirty Joke, Second Series*. Wharton, N. J., 1975.

Lockridge, Norman [Samuel Roth]. *Waggish Tales of the Czechs*. Chicago, 1947.

Masterson, James R. *Tall Tales of Arkansas*. Boston, 1943.

Mitchell, Francis. *The Wing and the Yoke*. Fort Worth, 1953.

Norwood, Hal. *Just a Book*. Mena, Ark., 1938.

Parsons, Elsie Clews. *Folk-Lore of the Antilles*. New York, 1933.

The Pearl. 18 issues. July, 1879–December, 1880.

Ramsay, Robert L. *Our Storehouse of Missouri Place Names*. Columbia, Mo., 1952.

Randolph, Vance. "Bawdy Elements in Ozark Speech." Unpublished manuscript, 1954.

———. *The Devil's Pretty Daughter*. New York, 1955.

———. *The Ozarks*. New York, 1931.

———. " 'Unprintable' Songs from the Ozarks." Unpublished manuscript, 1954.

———. "Vulgar Rhymes from the Ozarks." Unpublished manuscript, 1954.

———. *We Always Lie to Strangers*. New York, 1951.

———. *Who Blowed Up the Church House?* New York, 1952.

————, and George P. Wilson. *Down in the Holler*. Norman, Okla., 1953.

[Roth, Samuel.] *Anecdota Americana*. New York, 1934.

Sagarin, Edward. *The Anatomy of Dirty Words*. New York, 1962.

Sale, Antoine de la. *One Hundred Merrie and Delightsome Stories*. 2 vols. Paris, 1899.

Shaner, Dolph. *The Story of Joplin*. New York, 1948.

[Smith, T. R., ed.?] *Immortalia*. [New York,] 1927.

Thompson, Stith. *Motif-Index of Folk Literature*. 6 vols. Copenhagen and Bloomington, Ind., 1955–58.

[White, Andrew.] *The Bagnio Miscellany*. London [Amsterdam?], 1792 [1830?]; 1892 ed.

White, Newman I., ed. *The Frank C. Brown Collection of North Carolina Folklore*, I. Durham, N.C., 1952.

Williamson, Thames. *The Woods Colt*. New York, 1933.

Wilson, Charles Morrow. *Backwoods America*. Chapel Hill, N.C., 1934.